Better You, Better Friends

Better You, Better Friends

A Whole New Approach to Friendship

Glenda D. Shaw

ROWMAN & LITTLEFIELD
Lanham • Boulder • New York • London

Author's Note:

This book is based on personal friend-to-friend interaction and offers practical, insightful, meaningful, and well-tested ideas. However, no part of this book should be construed as medical, therapeutic, or life coaching advice—I'll leave that to the professionals! In most of the personal stories I have changed people's names—and in some cases moved locations or provided slightly different personal attributes—to protect their identities.

Published by Rowman & Littlefield
An imprint of The Rowman & Littlefield Publishing Group, Inc.
4501 Forbes Boulevard, Suite 200, Lanham, Maryland 20706
www.rowman.com

86–90 Paul Street, London EC2A 4NE, United Kingdom

British Library Cataloguing in Publication Information Available

Library of Congress Cataloging-in-Publication Data

Names: Shaw, Glenda D., 1955– author.
Title: Better you, better friends : a whole new approach to friendship / Glenda D. Shaw.
Description: Lanham : Rowman & Littlefield, 2021. | Includes bibliographical references and index. | Summary: "Shows readers how to overcome challenges in friendships with personal stories and examples by the author" — Provided by publisher.
Identifiers: LCCN 2021004607 (print) | LCCN 2021004608 (ebook) | ISBN 9781538152713 (cloth) | ISBN 9781538152720 (epub)
Subjects: LCSH: Friendship. | Families.
Classification: LCC BF575.F66 S43 2021 (print) | LCC BF575.F66 (ebook) | DDC 177/.62—dc23
LC record available at https://lccn.loc.gov/2021004607
LC ebook record available at https://lccn.loc.gov/2021004608

Contents

"You've *Got* to Be Kidding!"

"*When* do you think he'll be here?" a friend asked, topping up her wineglass. Unfortunately, I had no idea. A group of friends were celebrating my birthday at a trendy West Hollywood restaurant—colorful menus, brick walls, garlic breadsticks—and we were all waiting for Mr. Late to show up. His birthday gift to me, he'd declared a few days earlier, was treating everyone at this dinner party to their choice of exotic dessert. But he hadn't arrived yet, and we'd been there for a while now.

"Where are you? We're going to order our entrees. Call me, OK?" Another of my messages went straight to voice mail.

So, we sipped wine . . . ate the food when it came . . . chatted. One of my friends complained about her lack of work and, in an aside to me, obsessed about her current boyfriend. Another talked about how she couldn't stand her boss who, she said, spent more work time shopping and networking than she did on the job itself. Someone else bitched that the long hours he spent running around on his daytime production work left him no space for writing.

Each time the restaurant door swung open, my head snapped toward it, hoping it was him. I felt embarrassed that Mr. Late hadn't arrived—and hurt. He'd promised to be there before the other guests. He'd promised on his family's favorite pet's grave. Promised. This time I had almost believed him.

He and I had met decades before, when I was editing the entertainment section for a weekly newspaper and gave him his first freelance assignment. "You were the first person who really reached out to me," he once told me. "You made me feel welcome."

He was entertaining and smart; he was my wingman: never romantic but often around. Except when he wasn't—when he was traveling or not returning my calls because he had fixated on some new flame. "You know I go loopy for perky brunettes," he'd tell me after the romance had hit the skids and he wanted to pick up our friendship again. He always managed to wheedle his way back into my good graces. Maybe I was a fool for his charm. Well, I wasn't charmed now.

I got up from the table. "I'm going outside. I'll see if he's around." I wanted to leave him a message that . . . well, let's say I preferred no one else heard. "Hey, you're so late, you don't need to *bother* coming. I'll buy my own desserts. You promised, and you screwed up. So, don't even come."

He immediately called back: "Wait, wait, I'm nearly there. I thought the restaurant was someplace else. It must've moved. I'll make it up to you. Go ahead and order dessert. I'll be there in a sec."

Birthdays are important to me. The birthday celebration is a ritual that gives me a sense of belonging, somewhere, anywhere. It reminds me of the ties I have to my family, even though I left home at age seventeen, heading off across Australia's endless Hay Plains on a Greyhound bus to college fifteen hundred miles away.

Since then, I've spent only a handful of birthdays with my family. I rarely returned home. Either I was in the middle of a semester or living overseas. I've lived in three countries, eight cities, thirty households and counting—many shared with friends.

Birthdays always mattered. When any of my college buddies turned twenty-one, we'd all dress up in our fanciest thrift-shop gear and descend on an elegant restaurant, ordering dinners that cost us each a week's pay: eating frogs' legs or snails, tasting baba ghanoush and hummus for the first time, sipping real Turkish coffee. These friends were my adventurous, kindred spirits, and I adored them.

I lived in England for a year to hang out with a friend. On a visit to America, I was convinced to stay on by another friend, who demanded to know why, if I wanted to write screenplays, I would return to drizzly old London!

For a while I lived in Santa Barbara, hanging out with artists and with movers and shakers who were, like me, poised to leave this beach town for bigger cities. I still wanted to write movies, but I landed in Los Angeles in the middle of a writers' strike. Then, through many twists and turns and fateful meetings, I ended up as a producer for television— for *The Montel Williams Show,* in Los Angeles and in New York.

Through all these years and in all my various homes, I would receive gifts and birthday wishes from my parents and, often, my sisters. To keep me connected, Mom and Dad sent me photographs of my nephews' birthdays each year, beginning when they were little kids, wearing giggly smiles and pastel paper crowns, and continuing all the way into adulthood. There were open wine or beer bottles then, but as they merrily toasted their big day, the birthday boys still wore pastel paper crowns.

After Dad passed away, Mom called me on every birthday, but I knew that this year's call was probably her last. Dementia was making her forget.

So, there I was, standing on the sidewalk, outside a trendy restaurant, watching cars roll back and forth along Melrose Avenue and a traffic light turn from amber to red, wondering why this birthday left me feeling empty. I went back inside and rejoined my subdued little party.

"Is he OK?" someone asked. "Is it car trouble?"

"He'll be here in a minute," I said. "Let's order our desserts." By this time everyone looked as if they'd prefer to be anywhere but here. And I felt pretty much the same way.

My phone rang. It was Mr. Late, telling me he couldn't find free parking on the street and he didn't want to pay for valet.

"You've *got* to be kidding!" I wasn't even trying to be gracious now. "Get a valet. I'll pay the five bucks." I hung up before he had a chance to say anything more. I looked around the table and felt a jarring sense of disconnect. Why was I with these people?

Across the table from me sat a man I called "friend" who often, I found out, deceived me. I'd heard he'd talked behind my back and spread ill will about me when he felt insecure about our friendship. Once he'd bad-mouthed me to a hiring executive, which kept me from getting that particular job! Another time, when I landed a terrific job, he stopped talking to me for several years. Yet when we were together, he was open and friendly, occasionally shared his ideas and resources, and he was often fun to be with. But I didn't trust him, and when we reestablished our friendship, I didn't bring up the past. It was an unexamined friendship.

Sitting beside him was a woman who often canceled our dates at the last minute with some tired excuse. Once when I was in the middle of moving, she'd offered me a place to stay for the night. When I called to make arrangements, she didn't pick up or return my messages. That was painful—left as I was, sitting in my car with my luggage—and it was also unaccounted for. Another unexamined friendship.

Many of the other guests were working with me on a current television project, and I knew that it was unlikely we'd stay in touch after this gig had wrapped.

Just then Mr. Late rushed in, complaining that the parking sucked.

This was *not* where I wanted to be! Sitting in a restaurant with these people—waiting an hour and a half for a guy whose dramas were once again disrupting my life.

That's when I realized that I was in the middle of a major friend crisis.

RELOOKING AT FRIENDSHIP

In the following days and months, I found myself wrestling with all of this. I was a loving, reliable friend, wasn't I? I celebrated my friends' successes. Followed through on plans and dates. Called on birthdays, sent cards, gave gifts. Endeavored to tell the truth. Shared money when it was needed, if I had it. But what was I receiving from this group of friends?

It took me a long, long time to figure out that this depressing birthday experience was a gift—one of the most amazing birthday gifts I'd ever received. It was a wake-up call. Because of my response to this birthday party, in time I was able to move from feeling at rock bottom in my life to focusing the right kind of energy on finding and maintaining a group of loving friends—friends who supported my dreams and goals, which ended up including (defying all statistics) a middle-aged marriage with a wonderful husband.

My transition was a journey. I think of it as becoming a smarter friend.

I had to be smart enough to accept that there wasn't much reciprocity in the group of "friends" I'd surrounded myself with on this particular birthday. And smart enough to acknowledge the more committed, reliable friends I did have.

Once I started looking into this issue, I've found scientific studies that show just how critical our friendships are for our health and well-being. One study of nearly three thousand nurses "with breast cancer found that women without close friends were four times as likely to die from the disease as women with 10 or more friends."[1] A study of more than seven hundred Swedish men showed that having friends lowered the risk of a heart attack. And another study of some three dozen college students, outfitted with weighted backpacks standing in front of a hill, were asked to assess the steepness of the hill. Those students with their friends beside them—especially their closest friends!—perceived the climb as less arduous than those who were standing alone.

The friendships I had were not, I knew, improving my ability to weather life's challenges. My friends' behavior left me feeling confused; our history made me skeptical of them; altogether I felt estranged and depleted.

Clearly these friendships hadn't started out this way. These people were smart and creative, and initially they'd offered me comfort and support. There had been some issues along the way, warning flares, waving red flags, all of which I'd chosen to ignore. I'd been in denial.

But what emerged from my contemplation wasn't *Gee, they're bad friends. I've got to find better ones.* It was *What am I looking for in life? What is my purpose? Who are the people that will get me there?*

When I'm faced with a big challenge, I think in systems. I have to. I'm a TV producer, and each television program requires massive and meticulous research. This involves gathering vast amounts of information and also (this is the "systems" part) organizing this data in a way so that it becomes useful. I think working with systems is in my DNA. My mother was a mega organizer for various charities and the local Baptist church, and my father, a civil servant, worked with other public servants and academics on the earliest computers at The University of Sydney.

Now, my own life had become a research project.

The first step was to figure out how I got to this place in life. It was important for me to understand the underlying issues; otherwise I'd merely be shuffling around friends without solving the real problems. I saw how I'd made myself much more available to local friends. Listening to their struggles about launching their creative projects or how they couldn't find engaging work. How their love lives sucked—by the way, so did mine. Mr. Late had turned into my surrogate partner, which was probably not healthy for either of us. That's when I realized how those friends were reflecting back to me who I'd become in my life. My system breakdown wasn't so much about them; it was about me. I wasn't thriving.

And that's why I created my own Friendship Program.

CREATING A FRIENDSHIP SYSTEM

I made a list of what I was looking for at this time in life, and what I saw as my five-year goals. I have often led an enterprising and purposeful life, and this had not changed. I then wrote down the qualities I wanted to build upon, qualities I wished to expand in my life: *curious, visionary, encouraging, enterprising, purposeful* . . .

My next step was to make a list of all the friends I'd seen in the last two years. Next to each person's name, I wrote down what I saw as their top five qualities. This is when it hit me: There were five friends who immediately jumped out as exceptional matches for me. We shared these same golden qualities. What was most important to me was right there, in each of them.

Three of these people no longer lived close by—they'd moved away or I'd moved away from them. The other two lived locally, although in my eyes, we hadn't known each other very long. Not one of these friends was at my birthday party, yet these were my kindred spirits!

All of these friends were enterprising and walked their talk. They created exciting opportunities for themselves and had the tenacity to seal business deals. All of them had encouraged and supported me in various ways, by offering me either job opportunities or a place to stay. They were curious and adventurous. One went to an underwater shark rodeo (I kid you not!) and another had traveled to sixty countries, on six continents. One was a top teacher in her community, and another survived cancer with such a positive attitude it blew me away. They had each strived to make the world a better place, and through all their own personal struggles they thrived.

Then, as I continued looking at everything in a new way, my life took another one-eighty turn based on, I'm embarrassed to say, envying one of my female colleagues. I had always considered myself an open and accepting person, but now I had to think again. Here I was, envying someone I worked with.

I later discovered that to envy someone who has similar qualities or is in the same line of work is quite common. According to evolutionary psychologists, feelings of unfairness—which we often experience as envy—may have contributed to human survival. Evolutionary psychologists Sarah E. Hill and David M. Buss write: "Despite its reputation as being distasteful, tacky, petty, and downright gauche, it is likely that envy has played an important role in humans' quest for the resources necessary for successful survival and reproduction over the course of evolutionary time."[2]

I talk about this later in the book when I look at why we compete with our friends. For now, let me say that the envy I felt for this person was a huge help to me. It prompted me to look at myself.

TAKING A LOOK AT ME

When I looked closely at this enviable colleague, it appeared that she had it all: a great media executive job and a loving family. And then I saw that it was the loving family part that leaped out at me. This was what I did not have. For years I had cast myself in the role of the career woman: nothing to tie me down, always ready to pull up stakes and move on to a new adventure.

Yet was this what I still wanted? Well, maybe. Suddenly, I felt compelled to explore the possibility of finding a committed relationship, perhaps even marriage!

So, enterprising person that I am, I posted my information on dating websites and expanded my wardrobe beyond crisp white shirts and comfortable shoes. One of my friends hilariously reminds me of a clothing swap we both attended where I had no hesitation about exchanging some sensible blouses for a sheer, flouncy top and a pair of comfortable sandals for strappy high heels. The biggest surprise was how much these kindred spirits enjoyed and encouraged this new me.

Once I became serious about my relationship with John, the people I had gathered around me for that fateful birthday party began to fall away. Mr. Late met John just once and started reading a newspaper while we were talking—or trying to talk. When I attempted to introduce John to the woman who so often didn't show up, she canceled maybe seven times. So, I would say that what had been a problem resolved itself once I focused on what I truly wanted in my life.

And don't think for a minute that my being married for nine years means that I no longer care about friendships. The studies on friendship I've been reading indicate that, more than our families and spouses, it's our friends that make a difference in our sense of well-being—and in our actual longevity. Still, as one sociology professor observes in an article on friendship: "In general, the role of friendship isn't terribly well appreciated. There is just scads of stuff on families and marriage, but very little on friendship. It baffles me. Friendship has a bigger impact on our psychological well-being than family relationships."[3]

Even though we receive so many great benefits from our close friends, at the time of this book the nature of friendship has rarely been studied. A communications professor noted that we go to therapy for family and romantic partners but rarely, if ever, for a friendship, because friends, she noted, are voluntary, rarely exclusive, and not bound by birth or contracted through marriage. Comparatively speaking, a friend is pretty easy to replace.[4]

Even so, rather than viewing friends as interchangeable, it seems important to strengthen our ties of friendship. And I'm not the only one who thinks so.

FRIENDSHIP MATTERS!

When John and I married, one of my friends and her husband hosted our small, intimate wedding in the bamboo forest in their backyard. That morning, I was lounging around with my maids of honor, sipping coffee and chatting. Until, that is, I cranked up Santana's "Smooth." We all sprang up and danced in our pajamas—one in her leopard print silk, the other in her long, red flannels—singing along, laughing. Later, we scurried to the silence of the back room where—meticulously!—one applied my makeup and the other painted my nails. It was a deeply touching and intimate morning with friends, one I will always cherish.

Yet these kind of enduring, committed friendships are on the decline in the United States. And a consequence of losing such confidantes is that we feel lonelier and more isolated. Many psychologists and health care professionals have reviewed the devastating effects loneliness can have on a person's mental and physical well-being. The former surgeon general of the United States, Dr. Vivek H. Murthy, spoke on NPR's *Morning Edition* about some of the health issues that can arise from loneliness: "I found that people who struggle with loneliness, that that's associated with an increased risk for heart disease, dementia, depression, anxiety, sleep disturbances and even premature death."[5]

However, it's worth defining what we mean by the word "loneliness" in this context, and the late John Cacioppo, University of Chicago professor and founder of the field of social neuroscience, shed some light on this question. In an interview for *The Atlantic*, Cacioppo said that loneliness is not a sense of being separated from people; it's about feeling separated from the people you *prefer*. He went on to say that feelings of loneliness can act as a wake-up call because "loneliness motivates you to repair or replace connections that you feel are threatened or lost. So, people pay more attention to social information because they're motivated to reconnect."[6]

From my own wake-up call, I had started to see a huge potential in expanding my ideas about friendship—focusing on people with whom I had more common ground. I saw how friend connections can be made stronger, how friendships can become more committed. I began to look at the obvious drags on friendship, from competition and envy to rejection and derogation. And I examined as well my own biases and judgments of friends, driven by automatic, unconscious reactions. These are our mental and emotional processes and automatic behaviors that are activated in our brain without our even being aware of them. Like driving a car—after you've driven around for a while you don't continue thinking: *brake now, turn the wheel at the corner.*[7] These processes are like the software that runs your personal computer—when you type in a word, it sets off a procedure you don't see. Your conscious mind is the computer screen. So, for example, you may not consciously think you're being biased even though you can easily see others' biases. *Hey, I'm not biased; you are!* I wanted to know what benefits we get by deceiving or judging those closest to us. And so much more.

One of the things that most interested me was to look for scientific studies and academic research papers on the subjects that mattered to me in a friendship: reevaluating conflicts; overcoming feelings of rejection, envy, or jealousy; seeing past the issues around money; acknowledging our biases—to name a few. In some cases, I was able to find some academics who would speak about why they undertook their studies and about their own personal friendship strategies. And how to find workarounds in the face of automatic, unconscious reactions, how to stop assuming malice where none is intended.

Let me say this in a slightly different way: If I am a good friend to others, I will have good friends. Knowing this, I had become friendized.

• 2 •

When Is a Friend a Friend?

I have an unusual approach to friendship, and it may have something to do with my career in television. TV is an industry built on social connections. It's a business where friends hire, fire, and share valuable production leads or recommend each other for jobs. Executives rarely advertise for a TV producer. They're more likely to call their friends for recommendations, and then word of mouth does the rest. So, people working in TV have vast numbers of friends.

I *like* having a lot of friends. When I meet someone new, I keep an open mind. In other words, I approach everyone as a friend. Which is a completely different tack from some people I know—those who focus mainly on their families. I've observed how such people keep "obligations" outside their family to a minimum and appear reluctant to take on new friends—so much so that they haven't developed many close connections since their high school or college days. People like this say that new friendships are too much trouble—and it's difficult to find a potential new friend who is trustworthy. Or that they're just too busy.

One of my cousins, whom I'll call Olivia, was a little like this. (Readers should note that, for the sake of privacy, I have changed the names of all friends and relatives cited and have often tweaked their life circumstances as well.) Over the years Olivia and I would talk about the difference between our approaches to friendship. I've always had lots of friends, and then at the age of seventeen I started moving to new cities—far from family and with a need to make new connections.

However, beginning in her twenties, Olivia made her family of paramount importance in her life, and she built a life around them. As the eldest child, she was close to her parents and looked out for her younger siblings. She maintained a few very close friendships of long standing. This worked for her.

Until, that is, her parents had passed away, her own children left home, and her second marriage fell apart. That's when something shifted for her. Olivia—quite out of the blue—pulled up stakes and left her home of forty years to move to another city. While family—now her children and grandchildren—still remains a focus, this new life has offered her more relational opportunities as well, and she is making new friends.

She's joined a book club, goes to ladies' luncheons, and now indulges a desire of many years' standing to travel. She's gone on several cruises, and she has met a group of new friends to travel with.

Olivia wouldn't put it this way, I know, but after spending a number of years examining many aspects of friendship, I would say that my cousin has come to a point where she's exploring interests beyond her familial ties and is willing to reach out to new people who energize her interests and provide support.

Given the kinds of work I have done—not just TV production but also theater and working for a weekly newspaper—reaching out was never an issue for me. When you work with people, you get to know who they are fairly quickly. In television, I would be hired on to a production team, often with strangers, and we'd have to get up and running quickly. I would be booking and interviewing talent, pulling segments together, editing packages—and I'd get to know each person pretty well. I'd see who works amicably under pressure, those I can trust, those who continually gossip or create unnecessary drama, and the special few who are amazingly reliable and trustworthy and who exceed my hopes and expectations. And, of course, there are the precious comedians who make everyone laugh, which is a special boon late at night when we're all giddy and wired from hours of caffeine.

This is the upside of working with friends. The downside is that there's a lot of gossip and competitiveness. And with competitiveness can come betrayal. Yet even if a friend did do something detrimental to my best interests—like the birthday guest who lied so I wouldn't get a job—that person might still be a friend on some level. I still went out to dinner with this man, for instance, and had a very good time with him. I just wouldn't share confidences with him.

I remember a monk once saying that we can all love tigers; it's just that we don't show that love by getting close enough to pet them. Even though I approach everyone as a friend, I never forget there are tigers in the field. And with the tigers, I'm just a little more cautious—I don't try to pet them!

In order to support myself in this kind of differentiation, I crystallized my friend network by being clear about how close I feel to any particular person and by acknowledging the various levels of friendship. Before I get into this, I want to look for a moment at what friendship actually is.

WHAT'S A FRIEND?

The word *friend* is derived from the word *love*—which is extraordinary, if you think about it, because friends start as strangers who, through time, allow us to express our love. These strangers-turned-friends may come from family structures that are similar to ours, or they may come from quite different backgrounds, religions, countries, interests, ancestry. Whatever the case, we have the ability to experience and express love for each other. This is the heart of friendship, a kind of reciprocal altruism. You enjoy each other's company—share a laugh, send a card or gift to one another, treat this person to lunch or the movies, support each other's goals, celebrate their achievements, and reach out a hand in times of anguish or need. Friendship is being there for them, period.

Most of these things require a lot of energy, the kind of energy that I am more likely to spend on my closest friends. Yet I make sure I stay connected with many others as well. I love going to weekend lectures where I can catch up with my local, like-minded friends. An old friend had a book signing thirty miles away, so I decided to hoof up there to support her, even though I hadn't seen her in ages. One friend invited me to go to a plush twenties-style wedding with her on the *Queen Mary*, and I invited another friend to the Producers Guild holiday and gambling party. On social media I make a point of sending personal messages, rather than posting comments on their news stream. When a friend pops into my mind or I dream about a person—yes, that has happened—I send them a fun email or call them. It's meaningful for me to keep these social exchanges active.

In a paper titled "Friends and Happiness: An Evolutionary Perspective on Friendship," four evolutionary psychologists discuss several studies on altruism, which didn't surprise me at all. *Reciprocal altruism* is kind of like you scratch my back, and I'll scratch yours, based on how our ancestors were motivated to form affiliations to help them hunt big game for meat. And these groups also protected our ancestors from becoming prey themselves.[1]

Yet another evolutionary theory about friendship, cited in the same paper, *was* a surprise. According to this perspective, we form friendships because we are habitually involved in interpersonal conflict, and we need strong alliances in order to win. And *alliance building* is quite a different stance from the altruistic exchange. Rather than just joining to help each other, we're forming a network of allies who will help us succeed in our conflicts against other people. Beyond the influence of our close friends, here is a rationale for our forming larger networks, connections with people of varying levels of importance.

Evidently, it's a more intricate—dare I say Machiavellian!—aspect of friendship that has influenced development in the human brain. Two psychologists at the University of Pennsylvania tested what they called the *alliance hypothesis* in a three-study series on friend ranking to specifically track some of the ways we rank our friends: how we determine who is loyal and who isn't; who is on our side and who isn't.[2] These intricate mental maneuvers may actually be a reason the human brain developed its computational systems. Obviously, these abilities were passed down, because the people who could accurately rank their allies were more likely to survive in an uncertain world.

What I would like to suggest is that we're called upon to make the same kinds of rankings and decisions today, tracking our friend networks.

We have all seen alliance-building in our lives. We watch it being played out in politics, and we've seen it up close as well—in schoolyards, in offices, and in all manner of organizations—every day and all around the globe. It comes down to loyalties. In conflicts, we look for support from one friend or another; we give our own support to one friend or another.

The way you rank a person's loyalty is an important indicator for friendship closeness. That's why I was so depressed at my Big Shift birthday party; I had just acknowledged to myself that the people I was with weren't loyal, weren't close friends. Later, though, when I thought it through and reviewed my network of friends, I realized that there was an excellent solution: not everyone I knew had to be my very best friend. I did then what our human ancestors must have done so many eons ago: I made some categories for the people I'm allied with. I call it *levels of friendship*. It's what we'll spend the rest of this chapter looking at: the categories of friendship that can—believe me!—alleviate stress.

FOUR LEVELS OF FRIENDSHIP

So, here is a quick look at the evaluation guidelines I drew up for myself:

- *Essential friends* are my close buddies and confidantes, who share many connectors and keep my confidences; we really show up for each other, and weather stormy times. They have qualities I respect and admire, qualities I want to expand in my own life.
- *Collaborators* have a lot of attraction initially, because they often fulfill a current purpose in our lives. So, possibly, they're more temporary by nature. Even so, they offer something significant during a certain time in life and are often fun to hang out with.
- *Associates* are single-purpose friends who share a common interest: a hobby, sports team, book club. We're mutually engaged in a shared activity, and we find pleasure in that commonality. Yet there is less stress in these connections because we have fewer emotional attachments.

- *Mentors/mentees* come in two forms. Mentors are the guides in our lives—usually more senior or skilled, helping us through one transition or another with clear boundaries and a lot of respect. Mentees are people, usually younger than we are, who are at the beginning of their careers or life journey. I have found that offering insights and guidance for these young friends often refreshes my own thinking; it's a gift from giving.

This list is based on my philosophy of life: finding ways to become more conscious and honest about how I interact with others. A friend road map, so to speak. So now, let me describe these levels in greater detail.

Essential Friends

Initially, you need time, proximity, and access to form a real bond of friendship. These are not, however, always needed to maintain these friendships once you have established the deep compassion and caring you feel for these close friends. I call them essential friends.

I've known one of my high school friends since we were nine years old, but as we were in different groups we didn't hang out together much in high school. However, we both acted in a couple of school plays, and we played netball together. After we graduated from high school, our friendship shifted to the next level because, as it happened, she split up with her boyfriend and didn't have anyone to hang out with. So, I invited her into my friend circle at about the same time I was applying to various film schools around the country. When I got accepted by Flinders University, she decided to take a year off and join me in Adelaide.

I'd like to think it was my sunny personality that lured her away, but after doing a lot of research on friendship I realized that an important component of affinity is to reflect to them what they are seeking in their own lives. This friend and I have always had a similar life purpose, and our approach to life echoes the qualities I listed in the last chapter: *curious, visionary, encouraging, enterprising, purposeful.* All of my essential friends are like this. We may not see each other a lot, but it doesn't matter because when we do, we drop back into the other's life easefully.

Interestingly, the word *essential* is derived from *essence*, which in its initial English usage meant an ingredient that gives something its particular character. Originally, the term was used to describe distilled oils, the ingredients used to develop a fragrance, a perfume. This is a nice metaphor for our closest friendships—the "ingredients" that contribute to our character and that add fragrance to our lives. If, that is, we're open to all these friendships have to offer.

Once when a good friend and I took opposite sides on a political issue, we went to a small, quiet cemetery (neutral territory) and, as clouds scudded across the blustery wind-whipped sky, she and I walked around and around the little path surrounding the headstones and debated our perspectives. Eventually, we connected on some points and agreed to disagree on others. We then hugged and hurried home to enjoy a *cuppa*—a nice cup of hot tea, my mom's answer for all things.

Our friendship seems to run as deep as our DNA. On a level beyond our debate, I get her, and she gets me.

I think this is why I am drawn to the television show *Finding Your Roots*, where the host investigates the ancestry and genealogy of some celebrity guest. I am always fascinated to see how many struggles each guest's ancestors overcame, how many opportunities they seized to produce the celebrity guest who's sitting there on the screen before me, talking to Henry Louis Gates Jr. This show started me thinking about my own form of genealogy, a friendship genealogy.

It was humbling to acknowledge the influence some of my friends had on my life. Dana, for instance, is a friend from primary school who later moved to Adelaide with me and was a noticeable influence. After I left Australia, Dana came to visit me in the United States and shook me out of my comfort zone. At the ripe old age of twenty-six, I'd slipped in to being a den mother to a pack of undergrads at the University of California–Santa Barbara. I was finishing up a screenwriting class with veteran film executive and UCSB lecturer Paul Lazarus and was still living in student housing. Dana persuaded me to move off campus and find friends who had similar life experiences to my own—which was a fortuitous move: some of the friends I made at this point are, like Dana, still with me.

It takes years to build trust with a friend, and my feeling is, if you haven't been through a couple of calamities together, the friendship hasn't truly been tested. A friend I'll call Ava had a medical emergency and asked the woman she thought as her closest friend for help. The friend didn't help. She didn't show up for Ava either physically (by providing transportation or visiting her in the hospital, bringing a casserole, even mailing a card) or emotionally (by calling or visiting to offer moral support). This total lack of support shocked Ava. When she told me about the incident, a couple of weeks later, I asked her if she'd ever been through a tough time with this woman before.

Well, no.

So, this was your big friend challenge with her, right?

Yes.

Ava's disappointment was that she expected a lot more from this woman. They'd produced TV together for years on a number of grueling productions; Ava had just recently left the show they were both working on. What Ava hadn't realized is that this friendship only lived in the context of work. Outside, there wasn't a lot of support or connection. And that's the big difference between essential friends, who always show up, and the next tier of friends, collaborators, who provide a great benefit and fulfill a need within a particular context. When you understand the difference, you can find balance in your friend network. Ava never worked with this friend again and, not surprisingly, they didn't stay in touch.

Although I'm still in touch with many of my collaborators, I just manage my expectations, and that way I can fully enjoy our time together.

Collaborators

I see collaborators as people who fill a need for me at a certain time in my life and under certain conditions. It could be that you need a close buddy in your college dorm to ward off homesickness, you find a fun coworker to offset the insanity (or boredom) of work, you meet like-minded friends to go clubbing with on weekends. Young parents will form certain friendships with other young sleep-deprived parents. Or you might have a great rapport with a few of your neighbors. The list goes on.

Often collaborators start with a sparkly affinity, a pull to get to know each other. And even if you have the time, proximity, and accessibility, you haven't quite developed, or are not sure of, a deeper connection. Or perhaps, it's just too early to tell. Perhaps this friendship hasn't been tested, so you don't yet know if it will grow into something more sustainable. And perhaps it won't pass those tests or even encounter them. When I asked some of my friends if they were still in touch with their bridesmaids, guess what? Most said no. Not really. A woman I know who had twelve bridesmaids is now only in personal contact with one and Facebook contact with one other.

I want to add here that I enjoy these friendships for what they are: situational connections, which may or may not stand up to time. I call them collaborators because I think of them as friends who collaborate with me at a specific time, state of mind, and place in my life. The only danger I see is giving precedence to this level of friendship. This happened to one of my close friends, a woman I'll call Margo.

A sarcastic, hilarious, and extremely talented writer in her late twenties, Margo was spending her days working in publishing and her nights partying with a spirited Hollywood crowd. The people Margo was hanging out with weren't seeking commercial success through script writing; they were literati but of the Jack Kerouac variety. For Margo, this was a *big* time-suck, with a lot of intoxication and emotional volatility. Every week there would be some sort of intrigue and drama: who was cheating on whom, who was working on what, who was sober and who wasn't. After watching my friend live this out for many months, I reminded her that she wanted to write drama, not live it. I told her about a writing class I was taking through a university continuing education program and convinced her that she should take it with me, which she did. Now, many years later, Margo is an award-winning writer and a friend, and she's lost contact with most of the folk from that enticing Hollywood crowd.

My point is that at this time it was important for Margo to let go of those other friends. For her they were collaborators—situational friends—but their socializing allowed Margo neither the time nor focus to write. When a friend is no longer fulfilling a need, or your needs are no longer mutually beneficial, then it may be the time to allow this association to drop away. I have observed that ending these ebbing friendships can be simple, and can be done gracefully.

There is no need to push such people away. It's not necessary to end any association with hostility, frustration, or confusion. I speak about this later in the book, especially in the chapter on setting boundaries.

Associates

Some friends fulfill a specific, definable purpose in your life. I call them associates. In my producing days, I knew who to call if I needed an industrious, reliable daytime producer; a bold celebrity talent wrangler; or an exec in charge of production, who could be persuaded to allow a little "creativity" with a budget. This translates into friendships as well: the person you jog with each day; a buddy with whom you watch ball games; a friendly neighbor who goes to Toastmasters or a networking event with you once a week; a fellow book clubber or volunteer for a nonprofit organization, temple, or church. Such friendships serve a single purpose well, and I probably wouldn't lean on them for emotional support.

Take my friend Samuel, a fix-it guy. Among my friends, Samuel was an extremely reliable associate friend. He always showed up and fixed something of mine that was broken. We weren't super close. We've never spent a lot of time together, and I know that he wasn't hoping for that, either, because when we met, he was dating a friend of mine.

Samuel is a professional actor, but between acting gigs he supports himself by building sets and props at a warehouse in the San Fernando Valley. If his boss has a problem with a studio prop—like making a red, ten-foot-high fully functional telephone—who's he gonna call? Samuel.

Samuel loves fixing stuff. He builds, welds, and paints; he knows plumbing and electrical as well as the setting up and figuring out of computers. Once when my computer was stolen from my apartment, Samuel loaned me one of the twenty computers he had stacked on his bookshelf.

This computer was delivered and set up with the cables connected. Just like that. Once he told me that he loved fixing stuff for his friends. It's like giving them a gift.

Collaborators might provide emotional support during periods in your life; I see associates as being more functional. With associates, I am more likely to share a common interest or goal. Samuel and I had a connection through a mutual friend, and after they both moved away, Samuel and I had very little contact. When the circumstances change, these ties often do too—quite naturally.

Yet the associates in my life have been fruitful and affectionate, with fewer expectations and little angst because there's less emotional attachment. If they become unreliable, ornery, or untrustworthy, it's fairly easy to let them go. And I'm now more aware not to sabotage these connections by expecting more from someone than what this person chooses to offer. That said, a few of my associate friends have over the years flourished into something more enduring: essential friends.

Mentors/Mentees

Unlike most other friends, the mentors and mentees are asymmetrical friendships, meaning there's a power differential between the teacher and the student. I find that this cuts both ways: there are the people who help me and the people I help.

I love my mentors, in that tough love kind of way. They've been inspiring and sometimes even relentless in helping me move through the various stages of my life. I must admit, though, that at times I have been a lousy student. Once I complained to one of my mentors that she had hired a woman who I thought wanted my job. I felt threatened. Guess what my mentor said? She told me that she was going to give this other woman more opportunities, as a lesson to me. She told me that I must learn to become more self-confident, to accept that I had a lot of untapped talent, which would grow if I worked hard and didn't keep looking around, worrying what other people are doing.

For my mentees, it's difficult for me to gauge my impact on their careers; that's for them to determine. But I do know the impact mentees have on me. Mentoring younger people opens my mind to fresh perspectives and new ideas, and I'm amazed by what *I* learn, often quite unexpectedly, from these exchanges. Like the young student leader I met when I was a panelist at a college conference she was attending. Alice wanted to move her career to Los Angeles (close to where I was living) from the East Coast (where she was living) and asked me to help her achieve this goal. But after she visited LA for a test run, she seemed to dilly-dally on buying her airplane ticket, or looking for an apartment. That's when I asked her, "Are you risk averse?" She laughed and said, "Why yes, yes I am." So, I stepped back, and shifted my perspective to get a better grasp of her perspective. Instead of being her cheerleader for the big LA move, I listened to what *she* needed to move forward. I got her perspective. This way, I could nudge, but not ignore, her boundaries. Alice will make her move in her time, not mine. She's now working for an international hotel chain in her hometown, although she recently told me that she'd requested a transfer to Los Angeles. We're still in contact.

SUPPORTING OUR FRIENDSHIPS

Each level of friendship is important. Each is about figuring out what you can offer each other. At certain points in your life, this means offering emotional support; at other times it's sharing common interests or being helpful to one another in your work. Over time a few people will evolve into something more essential to your long-term well-being.

At each stage of friendship, however, we share love and acceptance. Just how much depends on our level of intimacy. As Oren Jay Sofer writes in his book on nonviolent communication, "Intimacy is born in conflict. Differences can bring us together and help us know one another. Friction can be creative and synergetic, leading to new ideas and perspectives. These kinds of conversations are characterized by very different intentions than our unconscious communication behavior."[3]

For example, you may feel that a friend is being unfair to you. We all know that feeling, right? Well, an inborn sense of what is due to us is just one of the attitudes and preconditioned reflexes we bring to our friendships. *Better You, Better Friends: A Whole New Approach to Friendship* is an opportunity to explore some of these "rattling the cage" moments and turn them into thoughtful communication.

This book is a reminder to exercise the all-important skill of paying attention, at any level of friendship. In the course of writing this book, I came across information that inspired and provoked me to behave differently toward my friends—like no longer labeling someone who caused me pain as *toxic* or calling them a *frenemy*. I found that these labels said more about my own inability to set boundaries or talk about unresolved issues, and that these issues were as much my own as my friend's.

Some of the studies I draw on here are recent, and their findings gave me a chance to come to my friendships with a fresh new attitude.

So, this book is about twenty-first-century friendships, offering some new tools and a few timeless suggestions on how to become a smarter, more compassionate friend.

From Your Friend's Perspective

$\mathcal{E}$very day we communicate with friends, and during these exchanges, we evaluate our friends with a different yardstick than the one we use on ourselves. Most of us don't realize this. We don't, for instance, see ourselves as being biased, but we often have no trouble seeing others in that light. Here's a little example. If your boss hires her friend, you'd probably think she was acting from bias, right? But if *you* hire your friend, it's not because you're biased; it's because he's a terrific worker, he's so dependable, he's highly skilled.

The difference between the way we evaluate ourselves and others is a blind spot, and it causes a lot of miscommunication and conflict in our friendships.

Like the time when my friend was nearly an hour late for a lunch date in Venice Beach. My frustration was palpable. The reason she gave was that she had underestimated the time it took to get through LA traffic. *Oh, come on*, I thought, *you know LA traffic. You used to live in LA!* So, I started this lunch date feeling a little hostile, a bit disrespected.

OK, so now fast-forward a year. I have a lunch date with the same friend. I can't believe how slow the traffic is on the 405 Freeway. It's a parking lot—and wasn't even peak hour! I hate being late. I am *never* late. Once we hit some open road on the Pacific Coast Highway, I pressured my husband to step on the gas, to weave in and out. We arrive at the café forty-five minutes after the stated time. It isn't my fault; it was the traffic. And herein, I confess, is my bias blind spot.

I judged my friend by the outcome (*she's a person's who's late*) and I judged myself by my thoughts (*I'm not someone who is late*), even though I *am* late occasionally. But for me, it's a special circumstance: parking lot traffic, a business call, got lost on a hike, my car needs gas, and so forth. My lateness makes sense to me. I know the reason for it, and so I don't consider myself biased. I'm just being reasonable. Right? Wrong.

Understanding such biases is an important factor in creating harmonious friendships. Becoming aware of these unconscious influences makes a huge difference in the ease of our friendships. Knowing the difference between how we assess ourselves and others helps us navigate a wide variety of issues that can arise in friendship. It's a friend-making tool at any level.

Matthew Kugler, an assistant professor at the Northwestern University Pritzker School of Law, studied this bias blind spot with Emily Pronin, one of his professors at Princeton University when he was a graduate student there. As Kugler explained when I spoke to him, "We know at any given moment what we're thinking, and we are very disposed to value that information, even when we probably shouldn't be."[1]

Basically, what this study found is that we have high regard for our own mental reasons—some would say *excuses*—for doing one thing or not doing another, and we lean on these thoughts in evaluating our own behavior. When we look at others, however, we are more likely to draw our conclusions based on their behaviors alone. Pronin and Kugler tested to see if this self-serving bias was, indeed, a "'blind spot."[2] As they note in one study, when students read about how most people "take credit" for "their successes as the result of personal qualities . . . but their failures as the result of external factors," these students would often report that they weren't susceptible to this kind of bias themselves, even though their peers were. And therein lies their blind spot.

I, myself, was guilty as charged. I had assessed my friend's failure to be on time as an internal issue: she didn't figure out the time/traffic ratio properly. I, on the other hand, viewed my own failure—*ahem*, lateness—as being due to an external factor: the parking lot traffic on the 405. In other words, I didn't see it as a failure at all; it was simply a circumstance over which I had no control.

We *can* use this information about the bias blind spot as a benefit in our friendships. "The recognition that the self is sometimes meant to be clueless," Kugler continued, "does fit in very nicely with the recognition that others will sometimes be clueless and that it isn't a character flaw." Which means, of course, that instead of telling yourself that a friend "is always late," you'll listen to her and *respect* what she has to say, because that's her own best take on it. This means you're taking into consideration what your friend told herself. To do this, I feel, is to do quite a bit.

This approach, in fact, was Kugler's next step in the research.

BIASES AND MALICE

In the first study, the subjects had no idea how the other participants explained themselves. In the second study, the subjects knew what reasons the others gave for their behaviors and *still* they continued to operate with bias blind spots. So, apparently, even if you know why your friend is late, it still may not appease your judgment of them.

I asked him if there are ways for us to offset our biases so that we can reduce conflict in our friendships. "That's something we were trying to get to in our final paper," Kugler told me, speaking about the fifth study. "We were trying to get people to recognize that there are limits to their power to control their thoughts and that there are unconscious influences. You can have bias without knowing it."

In study 5, half of the subjects were given a mocked-up article based on real scientific data about how unconscious influences were at work in their own minds—an article that had been allegedly published in a highly respected scientific journal. It turned out that it was *only* the subjects selected to read this article on the bias blind spot who recognized they weren't as rational as they'd thought. "Suddenly," Kugler said, "they were much less likely to show their bias blind spot."

As I indicated above, this can be the case for you, as well. Since you've been made aware of this bias blind spot, you can be on the watch for it. Whenever you go into a conversation assuming the worst—*she doesn't value my time, he never shows up for me when I need him, she's always preoccupied when she's with me,* and so on—you could ask yourself how your friend might see this circumstance. Or, ask them. Kugler admitted that there aren't any shortcuts or tricks to figuring out your friend's behavior. But the first step is your recognition that the gap between your respective experiences is larger than you might have thought. Your original thoughts might have run like this: *He's being inconsiderate, and he meant to be inconsiderate—or even manipulative!* Instead, you might now consider that none of this crossed your friend's mind. If the two of you could simply share information at this point, then you would be in a good place to avoid a hostile confrontation.

Kugler had an excellent way of putting this: "You shouldn't draw the assumption of malice."

The assumption of malice. Wow! That *is* something we do, isn't it! When a friend isn't acting in a way we'd like them to and we don't truly know where they're coming from, most of us can easily jump to an assumption of malice. And quick emails, telephone calls, and texts can often trigger our biases and prompt us to assume malice, just because we have so little information to work on. Let me tell you about a recent text exchange I had with a friend.

Ava and I had a telephone meeting planned, but when I called, she couldn't talk. She said something like, "My mom—" and abruptly hung up.

I had an automatic angry rush of *whoa, that was incredibly rude!* I felt dissed by her, and it hurt. Then, I stopped myself. I brought my reaction into my awareness, and I saw that Ava intended no malice toward me. My response was my own reactivity. She was the one who needed comforting right now, not me. So, I texted her:

Thinking of you!!! Sending love & a hug—gxxx

Two minutes later she responded:

So sorry I was so abrupt. Thanks for understanding. Elder care, a nonstop party.

My quick response:

My love to your mom & you take care . . . xx

Her immediate reply:

I'll call you as soon as I can.

Any misunderstanding, ambiguity, or residual upset was avoided.

Ava is one of my essential friends, so we have a long history of trust between us. Yet even with a close friend it's important to keep the positive energy in the friendship. It's important not to take each other for granted and not to take exchanges personally—not to assume malice.

Once we become aware of our biases, we can be less favorable in our own introspection and more compassionate and less judgmental in evaluating our friends. These ideas around our unconscious biases and how we judge another's behavior are applicable to all levels of our friendships. But how do we put these breakthrough concepts into action? How do I have that conversation with a friend?

THE IMPORTANCE OF SHARING INFORMATION

Nicholas Epley lays this out in his compelling book *Mindwise*. He writes, "Knowing others' minds requires asking and listening, not just reading and guessing. The gains that come from getting perspective directly instead of guessing about someone's perspective can be big."[3] Stop guessing, Epley says, because you don't really know what your friend is thinking. Epley is definitely right about that. I learned this on my own a few years back in an incident that, extended though it was, I feel is worth recounting here.

In the early days of social media, I had hired my friend Karen, who was in the process of turning her traditional media business into a social media branding and marketing company. I'd just written two blogs on friendship that were about to be posted on some well-trafficked internet sites, and I thought that marketing was just what I needed. So, on a limited budget and with a lot of enthusiasm, I hired my friend. Nothing happened. Which left me scrambling at the last minute to generate some traction for the blogs.

OK, she's new at this, so give her some time.

We set up a meeting to go over our social media strategy. She needed my passwords again; she'd lost them. That's why, she told me, nothing had been done.

Maybe we could work on a schedule together, set up a calendar, establish a rhythm. We planned that she would upload my tweets and blogs to an online social media distribution service. Afterward, she posted one tweet. That's it.

Over the next few weeks, Karen continued to go back and forth, back and forth. Still nothing got done. I became frustrated by her behavior, discouraged by what I saw as her excuses, all the while telling myself, *she'll figure it out, she'll turn a corner.*

Then she announced that she'd been up until three that morning, trying to set up an Excel spreadsheet. She had come up with an elaborate plan to repurpose my older blogs into talking points for traditional media. A project we hadn't discussed. Oh, and by the way, could I give her some more money?

Ah . . . that would be a no; there was no more money in the budget. But, why not keep the leftover money as a gift and concentrate on getting a full-time job?

"No." Karen was adamant she wanted to complete our agreement.

Now, what's a frustrated, baffled friend to do? I set up a face-to-face meeting to get her perspective in person, driving the sixty-five miles to her place.

As we settled in for our talk, Karen busied herself in the kitchen, making me a pot of Earl Grey, talking niceties, tiptoeing around our impending "talk." Then, with the tea tray, she delivered a bombshell: "My brain's scrambled, and I can't keep anything in one place. My new drug cocktail doesn't work, and half the time I can't get out of bed. My commitment to our friendship and what you're doing is unwavering. I'm changing my cocktail next week, so hopefully that will help."

Whoa! With my teacup poised in midair, I finally realized that we'd never discussed *why* all of this was happening: this disconnect between Karen's being a dynamic brand manager and the struggle she was having with the simplest tasks. We'd talked only about the *what*: the whatever-it-was that wasn't getting done. And I'd just kept on throwing new tasks and strategies at the problem, hoping something would stick.

Karen told me she wanted to deliver, but at this time in her life she couldn't. She wanted to make it work, but her own anxiety and severe depression prevented her from fully participating.

Her revelation shook me to the core. And my big fat *aha* moment was this: How could I build a friend brand when the brand was becoming more important than paying attention to what was happening behind the scenes in my own friend's life!

Listening to Karen that day had a huge impact on me. This was one of my big lessons on friendship. I recognized that I'd been biased—viewing Karen's unreliability as a lack of interest—and I fully acknowledged my friend and her struggles. I honored her frankness. We moved from potential hostile confrontation to listening to each other.

One experience, two perspectives, and a whole lot of love!

After our discussion, Karen admitted that this project was probably not a great fit for her right now. She promised to continue consulting with me on a friend basis—which she has done.

By sharing this intimacy, Karen showed me how to see beyond a friend's "unreliable and unpredictable" label. Before our conversation, I had been spending a lot of time on busywork like writing blogs and running a website. Afterward, I began to reflect on my own experiences and insights into how to become a smarter, more compassionate friend. And this conversation was one of the reasons I wrote this book.

It turned out that digging deeper into Karen's narrative helped me reexamine my own. And really, when you think about it, it doesn't matter at what level of friendship you are with someone, once you allow yourself to rise above an assumption of malice—once you take the time to see what is truly happening with your friend—you will almost always become better friends. Moments like this can make or break our friendships, and we get to decide how we'll handle them. We need to be willing to make that brain shift out of blaming mode; we need to learn to ask and to listen—even if it's uncomfortable.

HOW TO NAVIGATE CONFIRMATION BIAS

I admit there *are* times when it's difficult to listen to a friend, times when his or her opinions are so different from your own that they're hard to take in. What do you do then? A few friends have stopped talking to someone in these circumstances, others say they agree to disagree, and a couple of people leave the "elephant" in the corner—meaning they talk about other subjects.

During a recent electoral primary season, I had a heated, two-hour argument with a friend. I thought he was ill-informed and biased, and I based this opinion on his choice of candidates. Where was he getting his (distorted!) information? But as I'd just read the blind spot study, and I remembered one outcome of that work: *valuing thoughts, ignoring behavior.* So, I stepped back and thought, *Hmmm. You know what? I'm probably just as biased as he is!*

I decided to use my newfound information to address what was clearly a threat to this friendship.

In most election cycles many of our biases get revved up. It's us versus them, especially in regard to our friends. Your own preferred candidates have the *halo effect*, and you think that everything they do is wonderful. Other candidates have the *horn effect*—wherein one unsympathetic trait can color your perception of the entire person. We reinforce these beliefs over and over again, whether they are accurate, partial truth, or total hype. This is called the *confirmation bias,* and it's widely acknowledged that we tend to look for friends who support our point of view.

Anton, the friend with whom I was having these political disagreements, is a tech geek and martial artist, who calls himself a libertarian and whose Facebook "likes" range from Republican candidates and pundits to Monty Python and the astrophysicist Neil deGrasse Tyson. Although Anton and I disagree on a number of issues, political and social, he has been influential and supportive in many areas of my life. So, our heated debate left me scratching my head. I couldn't fathom why my friend would vote for that *other* candidate. Anton defended his *why*, with me muttering, "Wrong answer." *Ping.* Then I chucked back my point of view, and Anton dismissed it, saying my information was one-sided and that I should look for the *real* facts. *Pong.* Back and forth we argued for almost two hours. *Ping, pong, ping, pong,* until we were both too tired and frustrated to continue.

Breathe.

It was then that Anton explained his current life circumstance, which was very different from my own. He had been impacted, personally and financially, by what he called stagnant government policies in recent years, and he wanted change. Big change. Although his experience wasn't my experience, I knew Anton well enough to respect that he'd thought through his stance on this. And I saw, with some dismay, how close I had come to alienating this friend because he didn't agree with me. Anton and I still talk on the phone occasionally, not as much as before, but that's probably more to do with our busy lives and living in different areas than our political differences. That exchange with him, however, has taught me that an opinion is best served with an understanding of my own confirmation bias and making my points clearly, rather than getting riled up and angry.

Why do we get so emotional in these kinds of discussions with our friends? Why are we so reactive? I posed these questions to Matthew Kugler, and he spoke about the *minimal group paradigm*, which had come up in his study on group biases. "You find with people who are sorted into two groups that they will develop conflict with each other as you give them opportunities to do so." You could read this to mean *whenever you give them opportunities to do so.* I found out that this is a very curious and revealing little paradigm, indeed.

One famous study by the social psychologist Henri Tajfel back in 1970 demonstrates that even random, irrational, and trivial distinctions can lead to favoring one's own group over others. The Polish-born Tajfel had fought the Nazis in his youth and spent World War II in a prisoner-of-war camp. Having lived with bias, he wanted to test its strength in a situation where there was no history, no interaction, and no personal gain to be gotten from supporting a particular viewpoint.

Tajfel tracked the reactions of boys, ages fourteen and fifteen, from a grammar school in Bristol, England, in what became known as the Klee/Kandinsky study. For those who don't follow art, Paul Klee and

Wassily Kandinsky are two artists from the early 1900s. The teen subjects were randomly divided into two groups: one for Klee, the other for Kandinsky. That's when they proceeded to identify strongly with their assigned painter, even though, I would imagine, not one of them knew a Klee from a Kandinsky. Under these arbitrary conditions, the boys from each group demonstrated how even irrelevant social designations can routinely lead to favoring the in-group over all others.[4] In lay terms, the boys were often enthusiastic about their own group and insulting about the other, although there was no earthly reason for them to care.

I described this study to my friend Jim, and he burst out laughing. He had his own art story to share, from a discussion he had with his roommate in art school. "We went to McDonald's to dinner one time and started arguing about the two artists, van Gogh or Gauguin." Who was the better painter? Van Gogh. No, Gauguin. Wrong, it's van Gogh. No, you're wrong; it's Gauguin.

"I probably portrayed van Gogh as a loser who cut his ear off," Jim said, "and somehow that argument turned into a physical fight." Which only broke up when they saw flashing lights outside, and the police stormed in to escort them out.

Before this fight these two young men had hung out together and painted together, often discussing each other's art. "After this incident," Jim said, "I decided that our friendship would not continue. It was an incipient friendship to begin with, but after we fought, I decided I didn't want it to continue."

Of course, it doesn't have to end like this, as I will demonstrate with a story about myself and a very close friend. Let me add that this friend suggested I write about this exchange.

SITTING DOWN TOGETHER

Last summer, Nora told me she and her family were heading up to Redding, California, to celebrate her mother-in-law Libby's hundredth birthday. My husband and I invited ourselves along, much to Nora's delight. Not only had she and I been close friends for decades, but I was also friends with Libby. I've shared many a Thanksgiving with Nora's mother-in-law, feasting on her moist turkey dinners, the best I'd ever tasted!

For this special weekend event, Nora rented a large house with four bedrooms: three for her family, and one for me and John. She emailed me the details.

John and I decided that we would split the costs for the rental and cleaning fifty-fifty with Nora, to offset her expenses. We also decided to turn this trip into an opportunity to explore California's northern coast-line, so we headed up north a little earlier than the others. As we drove inland to Redding, I called Nora. She said that if we were the first to arrive, we should grab a room; we'd figure the rest out later.

So, when we got there, we felt it would be OK to grab the "best" bedroom—the largest, the one with a self-contained bathroom, the one that was tucked away from the others. We knew one niece might be crashing on the living room couch and lots of other relatives were com-ing over for various social events.

Happily, we dropped our suitcases on the bed and headed out for dinner. By the time we returned, Nora and her family had arrived.

As soon as the greetings and hugs were over, Nora told me, "I feel a little uncomfortable about you just taking this room."

I could hear the charge behind this comment, and I was right. Within moments, it was clear that Nora didn't think it was fair that we'd planted ourselves in the best room, so I said, "All right, let's talk about that." At first, she suggested we draw straws to see who got the room, but I didn't want to resolve it this way, through random selection.

So, Nora suggested we take this discussion out of others' hearing. "We don't have to involve anyone else, so let's just go outside and talk about this privately," she said.

It was a balmy summer evening. We sat down facing each other in a couple of garden chairs and went into our negotiation. Nora started. She told me that because John and I got there first, "I don't think you can automatically jump into that space!" She was paying for three out of the four bedrooms, she said, and so she felt that she should have equal say in which room she got.

That's when I piped in, "Hang on, didn't I tell you that John and I are paying for half the rent and cleaning costs?"

Nora looked surprised. "Nope, I didn't know that." Then she thought about it, and said, "OK, you've got a good point. Cool. Resolved. Done."

And it was. We laughed, we hugged, and we went back inside to join the others. We all had a terrific weekend, and Libby felt truly celebrated.

In all our friendships it's vital to find ways to talk through our issues. Whether your disagreement with a friend is small, like this one, or huge, it's good to give it the right kind of airtime—it's important to share your perspectives. We all want to be treated fairly. It's just that simple. This is what Nora wanted, and it's what I wanted: an equitable arrangement for the weekend. And as she pointed out to me recently when we rehashed this moment, neither of us at any time assumed malice. We both wanted to work it out.

With this in mind, I want to suggest that an important friend-making ploy is to discard assuming malice at any time when a friend behaves in a way that doesn't suit you—or when you don't immediately understand her motives.

Our biases with friends and our propensity to assume malice are, I feel, significant and underexplored areas in friendship. These two factors are complicated by another underexplored tendency we have with friends: competition.

Surprisingly, the closer our friendship, the stronger our competitive urges seem to become.

• 4 •

Anything You Can Do, I Can Do Better!

*L*et me start by saying that most of us compete with our friends. When I say *compete*, it's often a friendly contest, wanting to do as well as your friend at something or striving for something they have. When, however, you get to the point of just wishing your friend didn't have this skill or position or relationship or *thing*—or you make sure your friend can't get it—then you have stepped beyond competition and into rivalry. And rivalry is anathema to friendship. This is when you aren't happy for your friend who wins an award, gains a promotion, gets married, buys the dream home, or is invited on an amazing adventure to make pasta in Tuscany.

I believe that healthy competition is woven into the fabric of our culture. To be able to live a balanced life, we must be able to compete, for healthy competition inspires us to be the best we can be. When we're children, competition is in our schoolroom, and it's on the playground too—almost all sports and games involve winning and losing. It's about learning to be a good sport. And in any team competition, we learn to collaborate; participating in team sports has been connected to an ability, later in life, to make executive decisions and deal with everyday stress.

What gets in the way of friendship is not competition but rivalry. And there is a big difference between the two. Rivalry involves antagonism. Rivalry is when you covet what your friend has achieved. It's when you hope that someone else fails, whether or not you win. It's when you counter someone's success by making demeaning and derogatory comments, *to* them or *about* them. It's the opposite of well-wishing, and it destroys friendship.

Rivalry is associated with the destructive inclination known as envy. Envy—our emotional reaction when we compare ourselves and our success to another and their success—is a powerful response. I was surprised to learn that envy is actually hardwired into our brains—and females have our own unique biological reflexes, which until recently have rarely been studied.[1] These drives are hidden deep in our biology, primitive survival mechanisms that are often no longer relevant to our physical well-being. They can even get in the way of our well-being because these temporary responses can create lasting ire in the people around us and have a deadly impact on our friendships. Long after our feelings of envy have dissipated, the fallout from what we have said, or done, will remain with us.

Envy, I want to add, is not the same as jealousy, which is the fear of losing a loved one to a rival. Jealousy, which usually involves three people, can also be a disruptive interloper to friendship. We'll get to that in the next chapter.

There is definitely some connection between envy and jealousy; the target of your envy (or jealousy) is most likely to be someone from your own gender. Women are more likely to envy other women, and men are more likely to envy other men. Each gender is vying for its own gender-specific resources.[2] This is covered in the meta-study, cited in chapter 1, by Sarah E. Hill, a Texas Christian University–Fort Worth research psychologist and professor, and David M. Buss, a University of Texas professor who is founder and director of the Buss Lab, which is known for its research in evolutionary psychology and deals with many studies on gender, mating, and evolution.

Let me add here that we all experience some automatic adverse reactions to a friend's success. These social comparisons are part of what I call our emotional dashboard. To some extent these resentments arise because of what Hill and Buss call another's advantage. Maybe you envy a friend who is smoking hot and is always the center of attention. Or a buddy who keeps getting promoted—he *must* have well-connected parents! It's unfair she can throw together an essay—using *your* research!—and lands an A-plus when you had to struggle for a B-minus. You see these friends as getting the kudos, status, accolades that you yourself highly value and do not receive.

In the first chapter I mentioned my feelings of envy for an entertainment executive I knew, during my LA days when I was pitching ideas to networks. Whenever I walked into this woman's plush office, she'd greet me with a huge smile and a hug. We'd settle into designer chairs in front of her commodious desk, decorated with tastefully framed family photos—a handsome husband and two radiant teenagers. Her assistant would serve us cappuccinos, and my colleague would ask me about what was happening in my world. At that time . . . well, it wasn't much.

However, as I told her my brighter, personal elevator pitch, my thoughts were streaming something like this: *She's got to have a relative in the biz. She really doesn't have very good executive credits. How else could she get this gig!*

All my threat reactions were sounding off my inner alarms because of this woman's success, which didn't sit well with me, not one bit. She was a highly accomplished and talented competitor playing in my meadow.

We're more likely to have these feelings of envy toward friends or acquaintances who share similar interests or work in a similar field. For example, if my fabulous food blogger friend won an online Webby Award, I'd celebrate her success, take her to dinner or send flowers. Her achievement doesn't affect my self-worth. Yet if a friend wins an Emmy, now she's achieved fame and success in my sphere of influence, and that's a little harder to take. Or just imagine that your friend gets married and buys a gorgeous new home while you're sharing a cheap rental with your out-of-work fiancé. Your friend's successes are highly relevant to your life, and that's when the alarm is likely to go off on your emotional dashboard.

Let me point out that when this kind of adverse reaction arises, you're not stuck with it.

And that's when I rethought my envy about the big-time executive who had a balanced home life. Because I hadn't "seen" her welcoming and warm-hearted demeanor, her calmness during times of stress, and her extraordinary ability to balance a full-on career and children with a husband who also had a full-on career. This woman had it all because she did it all, through grit, attention, and warmth. I was able to understand this once I looked past my envy and the idealized version of this woman I had created in my mind.

So, I thought about this more deeply, and that's when I came up with the understanding I spoke about earlier. I wasn't envious because I craved this woman's prestigious job; what I wanted was the emotional balance she was living with. I wanted a loving partner and family as well as my career. Once I realized what I coveted, I was able to focus on that intention and slowly bring it into my life. Eventually, by analyzing my envy, I was able to grow from it.

As Hill and Buss point out in their meta-study, rather than just coping with envy, we need to address the situation that gave rise to it. "Just as the best course of action to remedy a toothache is to remove the decay (rather than developing coping techniques to deal with the pain), the best way to fix envy is to solve the adaptive problem that it is signaling needs to be solved."[3]

There are many influences—some of them inside us—making it difficult to accomplish this. But as we look more closely at the influences in our own lives, we can find ways to avoid enacting the fallout from envy with our friends.

FIVE WAYS TO COUNTERACT ENVY

As we've discovered, a rush of envy is part of our complex emotional survival mechanism. We can, however, experiment with various workarounds to try to offset the pain. Here are five techniques I use in my own life:

1. Redress imbalances
   The first step in dealing with envy is to figure out what's missing in your own life. Beginning to resolve those issues can help you reclaim balance. Like the time I envied friends who had the courage to move to bigger cities to boost their careers. Instead of thinking, *They'll never make*

it, I thought, *If they can do it, so can I!* And off I went, in my wood-paneled Dodge station wagon filled with boxes to launch my own new career adventure.

2. Work to improve

   If you want to compete in a healthy way, compete with yourself. I've had quite a few friends who are naturally talented writers, something I felt was an *unfair* advantage, because I was so bad at it. One evening in college, I got a reading from a palmist who told me I could be a professional writer. At the time, the friends who heard this laughed. But for the next two decades I studied and I wrote. I took college-level classes in screenwriting, playwriting, short story writing—and, eventually, I was nominated for a Daytime Emmy in writing.

3. Talk about it

   Communicating with a friend about your envy for them is a difficult conversation to have. You're kind of saying, *I feel your life is better than mine, and I want it.* One of the ways I like to do this is to run my feelings of envy by a third party, another friend. I remember having one of those unhappy moments when I stared in the mirror, and it looked as if I'd aged five years in a couple of months. I felt old, drab, and unattractive, especially compared to some of my LA friends. I mentioned this to my buddy Anton, who told me, "You're beautiful. Your beauty is based on your attitude, which comes from within. And it's unique to you; it shows your inner strength." I could certainly live with that! Of course, with this suggestion, you have to find the *right* friend to ask.

4. Get some perspective

   Seeing a photograph on social media of a friend flying first class to Europe or running into a group of people I know having a hilarious time together at a restaurant can leave me feeling a little left out—with a pang of envy. Then I turn to reason and logic: *OK, I could probably afford to go to Europe—maybe not in first class—but that's not what I'm choosing to do.* Or *I haven't seen the party host in more than three years, so why assume it was a rejection that I wasn't invited?* My dear friend Susan has a tradition of celebrating her birthday every year with friends in Los Angeles. She told me years ago, "If you're ever in the neighborhood, you're always invited!"—yet she doesn't send me an invitation. There are so many reasons why you may not be invited—and it could be as simple as not being around at the time. So, practice, practice, practice this common-sense perspective.

5. Focus on your goals

   Focus and refocus on your own personal goals. I keep asking myself, *What do I really want?* That's why I spend time doing an annual year-end review: a time when I revisit and refine my goals. For each goal, I write down five actions that will help me get there. It's surprising how often we feel envy for things that we've decided aren't a priority or for things we really don't want anymore. So, it's important to regularly remind ourselves about what our priorities are. It sounds so simple, but *simple* isn't always easy to do.

Now, let's look at how these responses of envy are hardwired into us.

EGGS AND MONEY

Another study conducted at the Buss Lab was done to gauge the effects of gender and hormones on generosity. The subjects were male and female college students; each was given a $5.00 bill and seated in front of a computer screen. The screen displayed a webcam photo of an attractive student, sometimes male and sometimes female, who the student had not met and who was allegedly sitting in a nearby room.

How much of the $5.00 would the subject wish to share with their online partner? Or would they prefer to keep all of the cash for themselves? This is called the dictator game, and it has served as a research prototype for the last quarter-century in gauging how various people distribute money under various conditions. It turns out that most people share between 25 and 50 percent of their money with their partner. In most cases, participants of both genders share more with a female than with a male. There are, however, some interesting exceptions to this norm.

Specifically, the level of generosity shown by female subjects' changes when they are ovulating. On average, an ovulating female "dictator" shared $1.10 less with an attractive female and $1.10 more with an attractive male.[4] Let me put this another way: before or after ovulation, the female dictator would give $2.00 to $2.50 to either a female or a male; during ovulation this same female dictator would give $1.40 to a woman and more than $3.00 to a man. And let me remind you: this is an *attractive* man.

Isn't it fascinating! I would never have guessed that my own reproductive cycle might prompt me to evaluate men and women differently—and to respond to them differently! Kristina Durante, an associate professor at Rutgers Business School who conducted this study,[5] explained that ovulation can make women competitive *with* other women and *for* other men. "So, when a woman is ovulating," Durante said when I spoke with her, "that's a signal of *I'm getting competitive.*"[6]

This is, she added, "a clear representation of courtship behavior: *I'm going to overshare with this attractive man and not share any money with this attractive woman.* So, it's a reflection of competition. . . . It doesn't mean that this is something that only occurs at ovulation . . . but it gives us an idea of the underlying mechanism. It's all about a mating motive."

And for most of us, we couldn't even be aware this biological bias was going on, unless we were tracking our fertility. "So, if you knew you were ovulating," Durante said, "then you could course-correct for feelings of competition, for wanting to derogate rivals."

If ovulation affects female friends through increasing their status to attract mates, how does ovulation affect lesbian friendships, when there's no sexual pull toward males?

"Lesbians still have those same hormones," Durante said. "Lesbians still have the competitiveness. Estrogen still influences their brain in the same way, so these hormones would still have the same influence in terms of motivation . . . they have increases in sexual desire only toward different targets." Obviously, more scientific research on how competition effects lesbian, gay, bisexual, transgender (LGBTQ+) rivalry, would provide a more robust understanding of human competition.

Interestingly, Durante pointed out that we know more about female competition than we know about female alliance formation. "We haven't really looked into this to a great extent," she said. "Women need to do two things. They need to compete with other women, but they can use other women strategically. The ideal strategy would be to have a select few women that you do have an alliance with and to trust those women. You can use that alliance to compete—almost like an army. Now you've got an army that you're using to compete with other women."

Most modern women began setting up their "army"—that is, making friend alliances with other females—while in their teens. Recently, I had an extended conversation with a twenty-something, the daughter of a friend, who had vivid memories of what it meant to ally herself with the in-crowd when she was in high school. It was a great case in point.

FORMING FRIEND ALLIANCES TO BETTER COMPETE

Zoey recalled that her main incentive for joining the popular girl's clique in her high school was to feel special, to be one of the in crowd. "I started asking myself, *Why can't I be noticed? Why can't I be cool?*" The ringleader and commander of this particular clique was a girl so outgoing and fashionable that everyone wanted to look like her—or, at least, be close to her. This girl, whom Zoey called the Pretty One, enforced a high-wattage sense of fashion within her own group.

"Everything had to be name brand," Zoey said, "and if you weren't wearing the name brand clothes, she'd put you down. I'd get to school, and she'd say, 'What are you wearing? Walmart?'"

The Pretty One didn't care whether Zoey's family was on a budget. Everyone else in her clique conformed to the dress code, so Zoey should, too. And when the Pretty One wasn't putting down her own friends, she encouraged them to put down other people. Anyone who didn't go along with her would find herself expelled from the Pretty One's group.

In time, Zoey woke up, took a stand against the Pretty One, and was pushed out of the group. No longer one of the popular girls, Zoey was alone. Until, that is, she began to explore her talent for visual art, joined the poetry club, and became active in the human rights organization Amnesty International. In time, she became a peer counselor for a program run by the school. By the end of high school, she said, "Lo and behold, I had made a couple of really amazing friends—people who shared my interests." Zoey forged her own way, not wanting to remain connected to a group of people who had what she saw as screwy values. Eventually, it worked out well for her on every level. She was even nominated for homecoming queen and ended up being part of the homecoming court.

This story ended well even for the Pretty One, who evidently outgrew her envy-inducing behavior. Zoey saw her again after graduation and found her to be a delightful individual. "It just took her a few years," Zoey said.

Name brand identification is not just a teenage behavior. As adults, and especially as adult women, we can go to great lengths in order to make ourselves more socially competitive—at times sacrificing our joy to be in the in crowd, spending our resources to have the latest accouterment of success. But why? My line of inquiry here led me to Jaime Cloud, an associate professor in psychological sciences at Western Oregon University, whose doctoral thesis (again, at the Buss Lab) was on how women signal other women through luxury items.

Cloud was cautious about drawing conclusions on why women compete, but she did surmise this: "I suspect that one reason why women are competing with each other is to gain status over one another. And my research is about conspicuous consumption—so that's the purchase of lavish goods to show off your financial standing to others. Like Louis Vuitton handbags, Christian Louboutin shoes, that kind of thing. Some women engage in this behavior of conspicuous consumption to increase other women's perception of their status. And in one phase of my dissertation research I showed that this is effective. So, the women who do conspicuously consume are perceived to be higher status than the women who don't."[7]

And, as Cloud explained, "status grants women, and men, privileged access to resources." She added that this is not simply human behavior. "It is borne out in the non-human primate literature too." She said studies among primates generally show that "high-status females get more resources, and their offspring fare better as a result."

I've always thought that these brand names were mainly about signaling other females. I say this because my husband and most other men I know couldn't tell a Louis Vuitton handbag from a Forever 21 tote or a Jimmy Choo shoe from an Old Navy flat.

But the luxury-status interest is no exaggeration. In one particular year, American women spent 50 percent more on fashion apparel than the U.S. government spent on education.[8] Of course, various cultural groups have specific arenas for competition and specific standards for success. I once saw a cartoon showing two monks sitting cross-legged. One says to the other, "I'd really appreciate it if you'd refrain from shouting 'KA-CHING!!!' every time you become one with the universe."

Basically, in the United States, women are competing with other women to look attractive—and we're competing more intensely with our friends in that regard than anyone else. Cloud said this stands to reason. "We tend to attract friends who are similar to ourselves." Laying out her example on a one-to-ten scale (with ten being phenomenal), she said, "Let's say I have an attractiveness level of a six; then my best friend is likely to have an attractiveness level of a six. If my intelligence level is of an eight, I'm likely to find other eights to be my friend." Our desirability level is often similar to that of our friends, and so they can give us some of our fiercest competition. As Cloud observed, "They're targeting the same mates, the same quality of mates, that we are."

Even though the architecture of our brain is set up to make us compete with other women, Kristina Durante pointed out that the social and cultural situations we live in have changed our needs. "The historical function was for access to mates and the resources that these mates held," she said. Now we're living in a different arena because, as women, we can earn our own money. Durante said, "We don't need men."

On the other hand, there are so many new ways to compete.

SOCIAL MEDIA

Even with a recognition of how primitive impulses affect much of our automatic competitive behavior, it's a good idea to consider what happens at that modern public watering hole, social media. Facebook, Snapchat, Instagram, and so on definitely stir up our sense of competition and can lead, on occasion, to downright rivalry. It's virtual, but that doesn't mean that social media isn't real. If anything, social media makes us more competitive with a wider audience. Decades ago it might have been a challenge to keep up with the friend next door; now we're competing with hundreds, sometimes thousands, of "friends," who are all apparently living highly successful, entertaining lives. You could see the friend next door in a variety of moments; on Instagram or Facebook it's generally only the most flattering selfies that get posted. Not the ones with a double chin (camera too low) or your eyes half-opened, which make you look disorderly, older, or unhealthy (unless, of course, that's your preferred image).

"I post pictures and add a status update whenever I have a major accomplishment in my life," Cloud said, "when I earn tenure, when I receive really good class evaluations, when I get some award. I don't post status updates about how my husband and I just had an argument or how I received a *bad* student evaluation."

As all competitive advertisers do, we highlight our best qualities and pitch any upgrade to our status. It's always the best of times, *rarely* the worst of times.

Because we all promote only our good times and achievements, that's all we see of other people—their best moments. We know our own worst moments, so we all feel like everyone else is doing a much better job at life than we are doing.

Cloud said, "This comparison makes us feel like people are better off than we are—and better off than they actually may be. On an intellectual level we understand that this isn't representative of their day-to-day life, but at a kind of emotional, intuitive, gut level our first reaction is to be envious of what they have—what they *seemingly* have—that we don't have."

This is a vital point: on one level we do know that our friends are advertising themselves. Nevertheless, it's easy for us—seeing the glowing, photographic "evidence" of their successes—to drop into feelings of envy.

Why is it important to understand these automatic emotional, gut level, reactions to our friends? "So our friendships will last," Cloud said. "One of the most important relationships in my life is with my best friend, and I don't want anything to interfere with that. And I think it's natural every now and then to have feelings of envy or even *schadenfreude* [delight in another's misfortune], at times with the people we love and care a great deal about. But we need to be careful not to let those feelings interfere with the good aspects of our relationship. Not to get carried away with them."

And, as Kristina Durante pointed out, "Now we sort of have this social world that's grown, in terms of how our brain is picking up on the people that we might feel competitive with, but they really don't matter. You know the Facebook friends that we have? And the likes we get? Even for me, I find myself saying, *OK, let's not worry about this. It doesn't have consequences*. Even though I might think that it does."

But even though it might carry an immediate sting, it usually doesn't have any real consequences in your life, either long-term or immediate. So, as Durante demonstrated, it's good to remind yourself of this—in other words, to reframe what has happened.

Herein lies the question: how do we shift out of rivalry into collaboration and healthy competition?

I heard an answer to that question a few years back from the wildly successful businesswoman Arianna Huffington, speaking at a networking event. Asked by a participant how she stayed ahead of her competitors, Arianna said that she didn't. She explained that if she's worried about her competitors, this means she's too busy looking around. She doesn't want to be looking sideways because she wants to be moving forward.

This, too, is a reframing. Instead of focusing on how well other people are doing, think about what's important to you and work toward that.

In the next chapter we focus on jealousy, another emotional response that can harm or destroy a friendship if not addressed. It can be confused with envy. In fact, they're often seen as interchangeable. But I think jealousy requires a whole new set of tools to deal with it effectively.

Jealousy

Three's a Crowd

$\mathcal{I}$ was sitting in my battered blue Mazda in the small hours of one un-
forgettable morning, watching my friend Emma make out with Liam,
the man I adored. Emma and I had been the last to leave a party at
Liam's house, and we were both supposedly heading home. But a look
that passed between them at the door had registered on me and, after
a few blocks, I circled back. And so, here I was, watching them laugh,
hug, kiss, and who knows what else in the front seat of her car. On one
level, I felt ashamed of myself for spying, and on the other—well, basically, I was shattered by what I was seeing.

When Liam got out of the car and chatted with Emma through the
passenger window, I quickly drove into an alley and ducked down until
she drove away.

OK, so Liam and I *had* broken up, but it was quite recently and the
trailing pull of *he's mine* was still registering in those deep layers of my
mind. And on some level, Emma knew this, because when I finally got
the courage to ask her if something was going on between her and Liam,
she said that they'd flirted with each other that was all. She shrugged and
said, "It's nothing."

I knew it was something. *Something* was happening between
them—even though it didn't seem to make sense. Emma had been a
great friend to me—loads of fun, dinner invitations, getting me a job. In
fact, she's the person who'd introduced me to Liam. Besides, Emma was
living with Eric, a friend of mine from work. That's how I'd met her.

For days I felt deeply distraught—which is the very nature of jealousy. I just couldn't believe this was happening. Then, instead of facing it head-on, I so internalized my anxiety that I began to feel physically sick. What helped to cure me, I think, was going to a doctor. I thought I had a physical ailment; the doctor told me it was stress. "Maybe it's your job," he said. "If you can, maybe change your job." Hearing that, I knew my "stress" wasn't about my job. It was jealousy.

Jealousy is not the same as envy. Envy is about desiring what some else has: an award, a job, or—yes—a relationship. And while this last may sound like jealousy, there's a difference. Because jealousy is when you perceive something is being taken from you, something you believe you already "own." Envy is when you admire someone else's happy relationship because this is something you want. Like, say, I might have envied Emma's loving relationship with Eric. I wasn't interested in Eric, but I would have loved to be in a relationship like theirs. With envy, think *two's competition*.

Jealousy goes deeper; it's more personal. You feel threatened that a person is being taken away from you. In my case, I guess I'd hoped that Liam and I might get back together, and *any* interloper was an obstacle to that happening. With jealousy, think *three's a crowd*.

Soon after the early morning spy drama occurred, Liam headed overseas for a long-term job assignment. All of his friends gathered at the airport to see him off, and a few days later, Emma asked if she could come over to my place. "We need to talk," she said. So, I made a pot of tea, the two of us sat down in my living room, and Emma blurted out that she and Liam had gotten together for a romantic tryst at one point recently when they'd worked together on a project. As she gave me the details of what happened on that one night, she seemed to be both embarrassed and remorseful. She explained that she and Liam had decided I shouldn't hear about this until after he'd left town.

I didn't know what to say. I was surprised to hear Emma's admissions and, I suppose, a little relieved to know I'd been right. I did feel heart-connected to Liam, however, and so the loss of him was still there for me, and I felt some jealousy.

Then a few months later, I traveled overseas. Part of the reason was to follow up on a huge job opportunity. But, quite honestly, I was also looking forward to visiting Liam and getting some emotional clarity. Which he didn't give me at first. However, I was staying at his apartment and when he went out one afternoon, I read a couple of Emma's letters to him. (Yes. I did!) These letters revealed insensitive comments about me, such as telling him, "Glenda's only there because you're there." to "I really, really miss you . . . looking forward to your return!" This is when the full impact of their affair hit me.

When Liam got back that afternoon, I asked him what was really going on with Emma.

He told me that he wanted to be more involved with Emma, and that's why he wanted to return home—to see if it could work out with her. "I thought she told you that," he said.

"Well, no, Liam, she didn't." This is when I realized that there had been a lot more going on behind my back than I had ever imagined—a lot more deceit was involved.

And this, too, is when I knew that my jealousy was spent. I was really finished with Liam. I didn't *want* to be with him. I had survived—perhaps thanks partly to endlessly singing Gloria Gaynor's "I Will Survive"—and moved on to a new life adventure.

I will say, however, that I felt betrayed. Had these two former friends approached me with more honesty, we might have remained friends. We'll never know.

A SENSE OF POSSESSION

In friendship, jealousy can come up in a lot of different ways—your romantic partner flirts with a friend, your buddy starts spending heaps of time with their new friend, or your BFF starts a new romance and pays less attention to you, and so forth. In each case, your merry duo has turned into a not-so-merry threesome, and you're the odd one out. Or, at least, you feel you are. The feelings attendant to jealousy can be excruciating. It's as if your very life were under attack. How can we work through these emotions, so that we don't end up spying on a friend or sabotaging a friendship?

At the time I was writing this book, Jennifer Bevan, a professor of communications at Chapman University in Orange County, California, was one of the few researchers who had studied jealousy between friends. Her master's thesis was on jealousy between female and male friends;[1] and, she later wrote *The Communication of Jealousy*, an academic book on how we communicate jealousy across all our relationships.[2]

"Jealousy is when you're threatened about losing something that you already possess," Bevan explained to me.[3] She added that we can consider an interpersonal relationship to be a possession.

It may be a little hard to wrap your head around a friend being a possession, because it sounds more like having a handbag than, say, a friendship. There is, however, another way of looking at this. Besides the obvious sense of ownership that usually comes with possession, "to possess" also means "acquire, enjoy, maintain, or be blessed with."

Although we are usually more possessive about our romantic interests than we are with our friends, still there are many stories of jealousy regarding women and their female friends. Sandra, a woman I know, a mother, related that for a while she was close with another mom, Sharon, who had a daughter of the same age as hers. After a while, any time Sharon saw Sandra with another friend, she'd become jealous. Sharon would make a comment: *Are you breaking up with me?* or *Are you hanging out with Patrice now?* And the nature of these comments was one of the factors that turned Sandra away from this friendship. The two of them connect now only through text.

Even though this topic—jealousy between women—hasn't been studied much, we have probably all felt a version of this sort of jealousy in our childhood and teens, and for some it is an issue well into adulthood. The fear of losing favor with someone you love or admire to someone else can be heartbreaking. Yet acting on this fear can be extremely detrimental to your friendship, whether you're the one feeling jealous or the one feeling besieged by someone who is expressing this unwelcome emotional response.

As Bevan said, "In our culture we don't really place so much value on friendships. A friendship is a voluntary, nonexclusive relationship. You're allowed to be friends with as many people as you want, so telling your friend that you're jealous of their relationship with someone else would almost be like breaking a rule of *we're friends, but I'm not your only friend*."

In her master's research, Bevan studied cross-sex friendships, which, obviously, can pose some different jealousy challenges than same-sex friendships (at least for heterosexual friends). Basically, these would be friends in whom you could potentially have a romantic interest. Bevan said, "There are a lot of romantic undercurrents going on in many cross-sex friendships, so we were, basically, curious about whether this had something to do with jealousy in the cross-sex friendship." In other words, there could be uncertainty about whether this friendship could turn into a romantic relationship.

This reminded me of the time when I was sitting with a close male buddy on his balcony, watching the New York skyline at dusk, chugging back beers after a warm summer's day. He looked over at me and asked, "Is this thing between us ever going to get romantic?"

I said, "No, probably not."

He smiled, and said "OK," and we went back to our conversation. Not long after, he met a delightful woman, and the three of us began hanging out together. That's a case when three is *not* a crowd—no one felt left out.

VARIETIES OF JEALOUSY

This last story was an easy exchange between friends, making it clear about the direction of our relationship. And once that was in the open, my buddy was free to date others without harming our relationship. But that's not always the case. I remember the time I had a male friend—not close, yet I felt as if it was slowly shifting into a possible romance. Until, that is, he met one of my friends and asked me for her number. *What?* I felt both surprised and a little jealous. My friend was surprised too, having only met this man once briefly, and having refused his request for her number. After that, both my feelings for him and our friendship dissolved.

On the other end of this spectrum, I have a friend who's rarely jealous and remains friends with all her ex-partners even when they'd found new romances—she's even befriended their partners too. And she once introduced her ex to his new partner.

So, as you can see, there are many variations on the sticky topic of the romance/friend dynamic.

One of the few scholars doing research on jealousy between adult friends is Timothy Worley who, with colleague Jennifer Samp,[4] has explored the four forms of jealousy we might experience when our romantic partner has a close friend.[5] These are as follows:

1. *Sexual jealousy*, the concern that a partner may become sexually involved with their friend.
2. *Intimacy jealousy*, concerns about emotional and communicative intimacy between a romantic partner and the friend.
3. *Power jealousy*, the concern that the friend may gain unwanted power or influence over one's partner.
4. *Companionship jealousy*, the concern that this friendship may detract from the time and activities experienced with one's partner.

In the first three categories, the partner has found a new friend who is of a gender or sexual identification that might be sexually appealing to the partner. This new friendship could possibly be seen as a threat to the existing relationship.

The least threatening of these four types of friend jealousy is the final one on the list. This kind of jealousy can arise when one partner has a long-term and preexisting friendship with someone of the gender or sexual identification that doesn't attract them sexually.

Even though the four ways of looking at jealousy are specific, Worley goes on to say, they are distinct only as concepts: sexual, intimacy, power, and companionship, because when we're feeling jealous we may feel varying levels of all of these, simultaneously.

Personally, I've experienced companionship jealousy in a few of my relationships. One situation, in particularly, comes to mind. There's a guy I used to date, Sadler, who was extremely jealous of my longtime female friends. Once when I was getting ready for a "ladies' night" out, Sadler said to me, "What's all that stuff on your face? You look like a clown!"

"You mean my makeup?"

Reflecting back on Sadler's comment, I see that this was just one of the signs this man gave me that he was jealous. I would say it was companionship jealousy because the time I spent with my friends was time I wasn't spending with Sadler. Yet, on the other hand, perhaps he wasn't sure just how close I felt to these friends—which could also *feel* like sexual, intimacy, or power jealousy. Had I realized any of this at the time, I might have been able to address some of his fears. I liked Sadler quite a lot; it's just that I liked my female friends, too. Maybe even more.

It is often hard to deal with other people's jealousy. The best we can do is to handle our own feelings of jealousy as they come up. So, let's take a look at what triggers our rejection response with our friends and some of the ways we can we deal with the pain.

A SENSE OF REJECTION

As friendships become more important to us, we may experience many feelings, including our fears around losing a close friend to someone else. For some, this can be as painful as losing a romantic partner. Why? We feel rejected. What I find especially fascinating is how the pain of social rejection—which goes hand in hand with jealousy—can feel like physical pain. When I was sitting in my Mazda, watching my friends make out, I felt as shattered as if the two of them had walked up to my car and hit me. This isn't an overstatement because from an evolutionary perspective, the brain's way of responding to social pain has piggybacked onto its way of responding to physical pain.

David T. Hsu, assistant professor of psychiatry at Stony Brook University in New York, has studied this phenomenon, and he told me that our biological responses to social rejection may have evolved for the same reason as our responses to physical pain. [6] It's a question of survival.

"We've known for a long time now that the brain's opioid system functions to reduce the response to physical pain," Hsu explained. Your body produces its own natural opioids, and these kick in at certain times to help reduce pain: "You've heard of a *runner's high*? That's when your body is in so much pain after strenuous exercise that it produces and releases its own opioids and gives the runner a natural high to feel good."[7]

What Hsu's research shows is that same opioid release happens when we feel rejected socially—our brain reacts as if it's been physically attacked and for exactly the same reason as if we had been attacked. It's a recovery mechanism for the body. For the human animal, both the physical and social aspects of our lives are important for survival.

Our survival is dependent on our connections with other people. Human connections are, Hsu said, "so important to us that throughout history if you were banished from society, in many ways it was equivalent to a death sentence." Our brains carry these same fears today. Even though jealousy may be a recent expression in our friendships, we can still feel the stinging pain of rejection[8]—because the emotions around social separation from a friend, family, or partner threatens our well-being.

"Any cues that we receive from the environment that suggest that we may be rejected," Hsu added, "even something as small as not being invited to lunch by your friend, sets off an alarm in the brain. And the alarm says, *Hey, something's not right, and you need to do something immediately about this.*"

I have a story to tell about this—the time I saw the pain a friend experienced when she realized I hadn't included her in an invitation.

This was years ago in Los Angeles, when Ava and I lived in the same city and she wanted to organize a big birthday bash for me in her elegant house. Ava and I had met in New York and both moved to LA to work on the same television show—and we'd remained close ever since we met. So, Ava asked me who I wanted to invite to the party. After I rattled off a list of names, she asked me, "What about Gayle?"

"Meh," I said shrugging my shoulders.

"No?" Ava was surprised. "Really?"

I considered Gayle a social friend. We'd been together through some bad times. She loved art as much as I did, and sometimes we'd end up taking the same art class at the local adult education school. On the other hand, she'd complain a lot about never getting a gig, yet when she got one, she complained it wasn't good enough for her. Once she even blew me off over a job I'd secured for her, which pissed me off. On the other hand, we could talk for hours about philosophy and relationships. At that stage, for whatever reason or transgression, I only considered her kind of a friend.

So, "meh."

A month later, at my fun-filled afternoon birthday party, friends mingled, laughter mixed with twittering birds and police sirens echoing in the city below. Ava's fresh homemade hummus slathered on home-baked pita bread was a big hit, along with the many other Mediterranean treats. Then we devoured a devilishly divine triple chocolate cake. Gifts opened, thanks sent, and I felt truly loved. Another birthday marked off the calendar.

Not quite.

A few weeks later, I went down to the adult education facility to register for a class and bumped into Gayle. We were chatting away when our mutual friend Fran showed up and thanked me profusely for inviting her to such a wonderful birthday party.

Yep, right in front of Gayle.

Gayle looked confused. I could see her thinking, *your birthday party?* With such delicious food, Fran went on.

Fran was invited, and not me?

Really interesting people, and—

Gayle's face turned bright red; she looked as if I'd punched her in the stomach.

Everything stopped for a moment. I didn't know what to say. Fran finally picked up on what was happening and changed the subject, asking about the classes. Gayle stuttered out something, but it was clear she was deeply hurt.

The evidence of my rejection was right there in front of me: it was palpable, and it hurt. I could see the emotional pain I had caused Gayle with my frivolous, dismissive, and thoughtless "meh." And from my shame, I learned my lesson about being cavalier and dismissive toward others.

Because being excluded, left out, really hurts. This is the reason jealousy causes us so much pain.

BREAKING THE CYCLE OF JEALOUSY

What can we do about this pain? And are our feelings of jealousy—which we now realize are part of our internal alarm system warning us about a potential loss—necessarily a bad thing?

According to Jennifer Bevan, the communications professor who discussed jealousy earlier in the chapter, "It's not always a bad thing. Jealousy can be a realization of your feelings for someone. It can be a way to understand that a relationship is threatened and that, maybe, you need to do something about it. And if you're honest with yourself about that experience with jealousy—that what you're experiencing *is* jealousy—it's acceptable to feel that way. It just means the relationship is important to you. Then, I think, that can reduce the negative communication of jealousy."

What Bevan means by *the negative communication of jealousy* is when we try to avoid revealing our feelings—which we cannot truly do. In those cases, we end up communicating in lots of nonverbal or indirect ways that get a message across but don't address the problem. Like my boyfriend who expressed his jealousy of my female friends by criticizing me for wearing "clownish" makeup when I went out with them. He didn't admit—perhaps didn't even know—that he was feeling jealous. And, as Bevan pointed out, such avoidance is even more likely with friends than with romantic partners.

The alternative, as Bevan explained, is integrative communication—the constructive, direct approach—which means opening up a dialogue with your friend. "You'll just discuss *I didn't like you spending time with that person* or ask, *What's going on with that relationship?*" Communication of this sort is both direct and positive and, as Bevan said, "That's the case across most jealousy studies; it's not just confined to friendships."

Unfortunately, because in our culture we see friends as voluntary, nonexclusive relationships, there are fewer opportunities to dig deeper into our friendship issues. "You don't go to therapy for friendships," Bevan said. "You go to therapy for your romantic and family relationships."

It's an excellent point, yet I think we need effective ways for us to work on our friendships. Because jealousy definitely comes up in friendship.

A year after my Emma and Liam experience, another close friend slept with my boyfriend—current boyfriend!—confessing they couldn't help themselves; he'd swept her off her feet, into his arms, carrying her to his bed. . . . Thank goodness she spared me the rest of that story! This betrayal could have easily spiraled into jealousy. Betrayal is something someone does to you; jealousy is a response that comes up from your gut to torment your mind. This time, however, it was so sudden that the shock of it spared me. Who needs such people in their inner circle! I just decided to leave them both to their own lives.

For a while after that I was a little more cautious. Then, something happened to reassure me about loyalty in friendship. I met a fabulous person, Cassie, and we became fast friends. She was artistic, hilariously funny, brave—producing her one-woman show in a night club—and (most important of all) loving. As we got to know each other, I revealed my stories of rejection and jealousy. And, guess what? The guy I was hanging out with at that time got smitten with her and asked her out on a date. I kid you not! This time, the story was different. Cassie told him she would never go on a date with him—ever!—because of me. He told her that he and I were just good buddies. She told him that she knew better, and, immediately after, she told me the whole story. She said to me, "I'd never hurt you like that."

You probably won't be surprised to learn that Cassie is the only one from all of those scenarios who is still in my network of friends.

And, since Cassie, I haven't had any more jealousy issues around my friends and my romantic partners—no more betrayal. It's as if my experience with Cassie shifted my understanding about friendship—about how a great friendship is almost as rare as a romance, and that they must be appreciated and nurtured, and vice versa.

Bevan agreed. "I think that friends are one of the main sources of relationship joy that we have in our lives," she said. "A lot of times it doesn't seem as if we have a lot of conflict with friends because we expect that friendship is going to primarily positive. With romantic relationships we know there's going to be ebb and flow, there's going to be good and bad, you're going to go through things together, and it might not work out."

My strong suggestion is that we take this same stance toward our friendships. With a friendship, there is going to be ebb and flow, good and bad. And to have a good friendship, we need to maintain it, to foster it.

"Friendships are really important," Bevan said.

I completely agree. Which is, of course, why I wrote this book.

· 6 ·

Money

Let's Talk about It!

I've always been pretty good with managing money—balancing my accounts. And that's why I was surprised when a friend called me a moocher. Not to my face, of course, but to a number of our other friends. This really hurt me; I thought we were close.

At the time, I was saving every last cent for an extended trip. So, I kind of *knew* I wasn't picking up my fair share at that time. But, as my friend didn't say anything, I thought she was supporting my adventure. Admittedly, my egocentric (and biased) take on the situation was that she understood my situation and was cool about helping me out.

After I'd left town, she complained to mutual friends about how I'd taken advantage of her. This was how I found out that, no, she wasn't at all cool with it. Clearly, she thought there had been some sort of boundary violation, even though she hadn't expressed her concerns to me personally.

Then, years later, I thought someone was mooching off me. I went on a lunch date with a potential friend, an expat Aussie who had been introduced to me via phone. She suggested we meet at an expensive restaurant for lunch. My usual mid-week workday lunch fare was to eat a sandwich at my desk, but I thought it was worth splurging to enjoy an expat chat with her. It was kind of like the friend version of a blind date.

Since I had to go back to the office afterward, I stuck to coffee with my meal while my companion threw back three expensive cocktails. When the bill came, she said, "Let's just split this." I was stunned. *Wow, that's not fair!* I thought. Yet I felt awkward about seeming petty, bringing it up. So, I begrudgingly paid half the tab. Don't get me wrong, I'm usually happy to pay half, but in this case, I felt I'd been played. And that's why I didn't bother pursuing this friendship.

It was only much later that I realized the problem in both of the above scenarios could have been assuaged by speaking up. While saving for my trip, I could have been clearer with my friend about how I needed to save money; I could have curtailed my social life in this time of self-imposed austerity; I could have risen above my sense of penury and said, "I appreciate all that you've done for me, so let me treat you to dinner tonight." And my friend, as well, could have said something like, "I got the last jug of beer, so it's your turn to get this one." Hearing this once, I'm pretty sure I would have gotten the point.

With my fellow Aussie, when faced with that bill-splitting suggestion, I could have said, "Sounds good. Let's split the food bill. But as I only drank coffee, let's pay for our own drinks separately. I think that's reasonable." This could have been a friend opportunity missed because I was unwilling to speak up.

It's odd that we feel awkward discussing this kind of financial exchange. Yet, this is only the tip of the iceberg when it comes to the discomfort we feel when talking about money with each other. Most of us are kind of skittish around this issue. We're wary. I've heard more intimate details about my friends' sex life, or lack thereof, than how much they earn for their work or have in savings.

A study sponsored by an investment firm in 2015 found that out of almost fifteen hundred women eighteen years and older, 80 percent avoided talking about money, even with those who were close to them. Women are much more likely to share shopping tips (65 percent) than spending habits (25 percent) and investment ideas (17 percent). Parenting, work, and health issues hovered around the mid-40 percentile.[1]

In a 2017 report, an investing app that surveyed more than three thousand American adults found that when asked, "Would you rather talk about how much you weigh or how much you have in savings?" 68 percent chose their weight.[2] (Ahem, not me!)

So, why do so many of us feel awkward talking about money? Well, it's possible that if we don't have as much money as our friends, we might be afraid they'll see us as unsuccessful, or inept with money.

My friend Jessica is intensely aware that she has to stay on a strict budget after paying off huge medical expenses. She knows how it feels to be the one who can't pick up half of the dinner tab. Yet, she wants her friends to feel comfortable when they set up a date with her, which means she has to be proactive. Like the times when one of her wealthier friends asks to get together, Jessica will say, "Bring your dog over, and we'll go for a walk on the beach." As she explained it to me, this way there's no cash involved and Jessica can enjoy a friend's company without spending money or allowing her friend to pay her way.

If we're wealthier than our friends, it's possible we don't want to attract their envy—or leave them feeling that they're not doing as well as they should be. Or maybe we're afraid they'll want us to pick up more tabs, pay for more tickets, ask us for a loan, and so on.

A woman I know shared her experience about how one friend used to always leave her wallet at home. This woman would bring just enough money to handle what they were planning to do—and when (so often!) something unplanned came up, she'd want to borrow money. Just a little. Then, because she had a terrible memory, she'd forget. "And I didn't want to *have* to remind her," my friend said. "After this happened a few times, I stopped loaning her money. Sometimes I would *give* her the money; sometimes I just wouldn't be there for her." After that, her friend started carrying her wallet. So, this is a way to communicate through our actions, and it's also another way to stop enabling a friend's behavior.

Being fair with friends in money matters starts by being fair with yourself.

And really, whether or not you're on a budget, what's important is hanging out with your friends, and we can all find ways to share fun, novel experiences together rather than getting hung up on the cost. In the book, *Happy Money: The Science of Smarter Spending*, two academics— Elizabeth Dunn, a psychology professor from the University of British Columbia, and Michael Norton, a Harvard marketing professor—cite studies that show how we're more likely to find happiness in a dinner out with friends, road trips, visiting a museum—than buying a new purse, iPad, or computer.[3]

Apparently, we'd prefer to have more time on our hands than money in our pockets—the book calls this *time affluence*.[4] It's pretty unlikely you'll have a digital photo album full of the purses you've bought over the last twenty years—even if they're Louis Vuitton's! But you *are* likely to keep pictures of that crazy road trip you took with friends, birthdays in backyards, hanging out anywhere or at any time in nature, dancing at any and all holiday events, and a lot of goofy smiles (especially if they're your friends' goofy smiles)—because these are the snapshots from our lives, records of our beautiful experiences together, our memories.

That said, I want to mention another potentially sticky situation that comes up between friends: borrowing or lending money.

LOAN AWARENESS

In this section we talk about small, friend-to-friend loans and not issues around investing in a friend's financial enterprise. For these, there are many resources to help you decide whether to invest or to give a friend a large amount of money—$15,000 plus—both have tax implications in the United States.

Yet over time the smaller amounts can add up and can send a friendship into a tailspin. My cousin Michael loaned quite a bit of money to some close friends of his, a married couple he had known for some time. "It started off very casually," Michael said, "an ad hoc arrangement. They needed something to tide them over till the end of the month." This turned out, however, to be more than a one-off occurrence. It even began to be regular: $80.00 to $100.00 here, another $200.00 there. Michael kept a tally, but he saw no reason to make this a formal arrangement. And, he admitted, "I didn't ask for it back."

His friendship with this couple had been pretty trouble free until finances crept in—and the amount involved began growing. The tally went up, and after a while it was well into the thousands. This had been going on for a few years before Michael reached his tipping point; he said no to a request for money. Still, they asked again. When Michael said no again, they stopped seeing each other for a while. "I needed time to feel confident that they really did understand that no meant no."

In retrospect, Michael realized that giving this couple money in this way was "almost like mixing two kinds of relationships"—a friendship and a financial arrangement. Now, if a friend asks him for money, Michael says no from the outset. "I'm not willing to go down this road. Because it's going to be damaging to our friendship." It also costs money. With this particular couple, my cousin never did get his money back, although they did slowly heal their relationship.

Most of the articles on borrowing between friends that I found online tell similar tales of woe. People who loaned to, or borrowed from, their friends often say that it turned into a nightmare—or, at least, it turned into an unpleasant experience that eroded or ended a friendship. An American proverb warns would-be borrowers, "Before borrowing money from a friend, decide which you need most." And Benjamin Franklin warns would-be lenders, "Creditors have better memories than debtors."

Although there *is* something to Franklin's perspective—I'll get to that in a moment—I want to suggest we rethink this topic. Throughout this book, we've been discussing how our friends are growing in importance in our lives, so how can we now rise to the occasion of making intelligent, yet generous, money decisions involving friends? Once we understand the value of our friendships, I would say the rest is about figuring out the math.

The first step in figuring out the math is *realizing that you need math*!

One online study that asked U.S. respondents to list their most recent loan—given or received—extrapolated that, from the people who responded, $184 billion had been borrowed in what they termed "friends and family" loans. It's difficult to assess the validity of this figure, but I found the reasons given for these loans most instructive: utilities and bills (46 percent), rent (23 percent), and medical emergencies (17 percent).[5]

Clearly, when our friends need money for basic amenities—survival stuff!—we feel a sense of duty to help them out even while we may feel a simultaneous reluctance to come forward with that help. The *Happy Money* authors note: "Googling *awkward loan requests* gets about 90 million hits."[6]

So it's important to untangle these awkward requests and see them in a new perspective.

There is very little academic research on what happens when we borrow from or loan money to a friend. One of the few studies I found on this topic is an investigation whose findings seemed to back up Benjamin Franklin's claim—except that, being academics, the researchers were more diplomatic than Franklin in their wording. The issue this study raised was how two people—the borrower and the lender—can have radically different perceptions about the same event, the loan. Especially when the loan is delinquent.[7]

The idea was to focus on loans between people with equal status and power in the relationship, and so they were less interested in the loans between parents or grandparents and their offspring. As it turned out, roughly half of these loans were between friends, and even the others between siblings or cousins were, the authors observed, of a similar dynamic to a friendship loan.[8]

I find it intriguing that a good percentage of these loans—60 percent—were paid back on time, and that this favorable outcome apparently strengthened the bonds of friendship between these people, increasing both their mutual trust and feelings of loyalty.

That's what happened the time I loaned a friend a month's rent. This request came up right after I'd had a bit of a disaster with another friend, who owed me money from a business deal that went badly—money it took me six years to get back!

So, even though I was happy to lend this second friend the money for rent, I asked her to put it into writing. "I feel weird about asking this," I told her, "but would you mind signing a letter of agreement just so we can formalize the loan?" I gave her a couple of years to pay it off, interest free—but I wanted a record that it had happened.

My friend readily agreed. "Just write up something," she said. "I'll sign it." Which she did—and then paid me back within a month.

As I said, this exchange did promote a great deal of goodwill and trust between us, and from this and other experiences, she remains one of my essential friends to this day.

But back to the survey. What about the other 40 percent of these loans, the not-so-trustworthy borrowers who were delinquent? This survey defined "delinquent loan" as one in which the payback date had been missed. In this crucial time the difference between the lenders' and borrows' memories kicks in. Of the borrowers, 87 percent were confident that they would pay back the money; of the lenders, only 35 percent thought they'd ever see their money again.[9] This is a big disparity—a whopping 52 percent!

I want to point out that this difference doesn't speak to the reality of whether the loan will ever be repaid. What it illustrates is a disparity between the attitudes borrowers and lenders have toward a friendship loan. The due date passes, and the borrower is likely to be relaxed, thinking everything is fine; the lender is likely to be upset, thinking they've lost their money forever.

A DIFFERENCE IN PERSPECTIVE

Let's take a closer look at how often friendship loans are made. Often, we jump in to help a friend without thinking it through, sometimes without knowing if it's something we can afford. Whether we can afford it or not, in that momentary feeling of goodwill, we fail to clarify the terms for repayment. That's what had happened to the borrower/lender study's coauthor, Linda Dezsö. She shared her personal story, which is what launched this study. "I had a good friend, Nina," Dezsö said. "Nina had many boyfriends, and a complicated life—raising two kids alone, always short of money. But, a very cool girl."[10] So, when Dezsö inherited some money from her grandmother, she loaned a large portion of it to Nina, who promised repayment in three months. She didn't do it. Then another three months went by. Then another.

When a borrower misses their due date, that's when their blind spot kicks in. This self-serving bias helps them believe the following:

- *I don't recall that the repayment date has passed.*
- *I've already paid back that loan.*
- *Didn't she initiate giving me the money? Wasn't it meant to be a gift?*
- *I'm going to pay back the loan—eventually!*

When a lender's payment deadline passes, their self-serving biases kick in, helping them believe something entirely different:

- *He is avoiding me because of the loan.*
- *The due date has passed; I'll probably never see that money again.*
- *We're not so close anymore, and it's because of this loan.*
- *She must feel very guilty about not paying me back.*

Since the borrower thinks they *will* pay the money back—or that it was a gift—they feel a lot less guilty than the lender would have thought.

If you are still wondering why it's a good idea to have a written agreement on a friendship loan, just go back and reread those two lists of reactions. They are so very different. The nice thing about having something in writing is that the amount, the dates, the payback expectations are all right there, in black and white. Having it in writing is a good idea no matter which side of the loan you're on—the lender or the borrower. Let's look at this from both perspectives:

The Borrower

If you're going through a tough time or are cash-strapped, it can feel natural to turn to a close friend for help. Remember, friend loans, if not delinquent, can increase trust and strengthen your bonds. Yet, let's face it, your friend's biggest fears are that the loan may not be repaid and the friendship will go belly-up. So make sure you create security around this loan by suggesting that the two of you devise a repayment agreement—even if your friend says, *Oh, no, no, I trust you!* it's important that you're proactive.

If you don't have an agreement then it's much more likely that you'll experience what my borrowing buddy complained to me about: "Two minutes after they give me the money, before I've even had a chance to get it in the bank, they're wondering when I'm going to pay them back." Reassure them; then follow through.

Also, as a borrower you don't have to feel more indebted to your friend or ruminate over how you're less successful than they are. This is a business transaction—and, if you think about it, your friend may possibly have a loan with a bank.

And if your friend says no to a loan, even though *no* is always a hard word to hear, bear in mind that sometimes a friend just can't help you out. They may be on a tight budget and have lots of their own expenses. This might be outside their financial comfort zone right now. Or they might have been burned in the past and have a personal philosophy about never lending money. Whatever the reason, it's rarely a commentary on your character.

The Lender

It's unlikely you're always going to say yes. Once a friend asked me for money, and I wasn't able to give or loan her money at that time. So, I said, "I'm really sorry, but it's not in my budget right now," which was the truth. Then I told her, "If my circumstances change, I'll let you know." Even though it's hard to say no to a friend going through a tough time, it's equally important to be fiscally responsible to yourself. And there are some friends in my life who I know are not fiscally responsible. I might give them some cash to help them in a pinch, but I would make it clear that this is a one-time-only event.

When I loan money, I usually ask the person to sign for it—especially if I know I'll need the money later. I'll admit that it's difficult to ask a friend to sign an agreement, especially when they're already upset about their finances. We all want to be the good guy, right! We'd all love to rely on an agreement based on a handshake! Unfortunately, if you want your money back, you need more than just a handshake. Think of a written agreement as an insurance policy, because if you're one of the 8 percent with an IOU, a written agreement, then your memories are 100 percent consistent.

And these days it's easy to formalize an agreement. There are numerous legitimate online websites that have itemized templates and even payment tracking for these person-to-person agreements—and these, I may add, are also legally binding. Many such sites provide a concierge service as well, taking on the role of sending reminders and requesting payments. For your friend, this might be better as well because third-party emails are not as awkward as reminders from a friend. (These sites serve two parties who know each other—not to be confused with other sites that offer loans through a third, unknown, party.)

Regardless of how you move money from person to person—whether via apps like Venmo and Zelle, in which money can be transferred or received immediately, or through more tradition means—these transfers don't address the terms of agreement for your loan.

As one of the CEOs from an online company that processes these services told me, "We're that third party that helps you legitimize a loan. We're the alternative to *Hey, I decided to give you money and here's the amount on a napkin!* and then hope for the best."

Linda Dezsö, who relied on a verbal agreement based on trust, decided to let go of her anxiety, trusted that her friend would repay her, and *did* get her money back. It just took a while.

TIPS ON LOANING TO A FRIEND

I asked Sharon Cox, a money coach for women with thirty years of experience in finance, to offer some advice about how to create a loan agreement between friends. "The more open your communication is," she said, "the more opportunity for the friendship to stay intact."[11] Friends start by building a relational "contract"—we share our lives, stories, confidences—and then, if money changes hands, we have a temporary business relationship. The relational contract is foremost because you wouldn't ask that person for money if you weren't friends; the business contract is secondary.

"But we still want to bring the business aspect into this discussion about loans," Cox explained, "and we don't know how to do that very well. When it comes to a loan, it's *whoa*, this is really upping the game, isn't it!" Often at such times we feel that we're walking on thin ice.

To avoid the discomfort of this situation, we laid out a simple friend scenario to show you the best way to approach a loan request: Ivy really wants to go on a reunion trip with some of her high school buddies. Since she just moved into a new apartment, she doesn't have enough money for the airfare. So Ivy asks her good friend, Simone, to lend her $300.00. How can this turn into a successful transaction? Once again, we've broken this down into the two perspectives.

The Lender

1. Ask yourself, *Do I have sufficient discretionary money? What do I miss out on by loaning this money to Ivy?*
2. Define the terms of agreement that work for *you*. Be clear, and clarify your terms:
   - When would you like the loan to be paid back? (I would appreciate a repayment by this date.)
   - Ask Ivy if this date is workable. Then, if necessary, negotiate something that works for you both.
   - Develop a payment plan together. Will it be paid back in one lump sum, and if not, set out an installment plan—$100.00 per month, for example.
3. Also, discuss the *what ifs*, such as, three months are up and Ivy still hasn't made one payment. Make these *what ifs* part of the negotiation.
4. Once you both agree to the terms, write them down clearly, both sign and keep a copy.
5. Then, after your agreement, keep your lips zipped. Keeping this confidential says a lot about your integrity.

The Borrower

1. Ask yourself, *Can I pay back the money I'm asking for?* Map out your income/expenses: How long do you really need to pay the

loan back? Instead of three months, do you need four months? Think ahead, prepare, so that you'll be clear going into an agreement.

2. Your friend—in this case, Simone—has every right to define the terms, but you can negotiate. You can, for instance, ask her to extend the time frame; or, you may prefer to pay it back in one lump sum, rather than installments. Be honest with yourself, and ask questions like these:

   - Is what you've negotiated workable for you? (If it's not, don't agree.)
   - Ask your friend, "Do I owe you anything more than the loan money and my appreciation and gratitude?" You don't want to get into a situation where you feel that you've got to help out your friend in other ways, because you owe her money—unless it's agreed upon in the deal.

3. Discuss your *what ifs*—if, for instance, you can't meet the deadline or other terms. Again, the clearer the better. Then, sign and keep a copy.

4. Stick to your payment plan, unless something critical arises. Don't wait to be asked for payments; be proactive from the start. And if something critical does arise, have a conversation immediately, well before the deadline. Ask for an extension or renegotiate the terms for the agreement.

5. Once you've paid back the loan, acknowledge Simone's generosity. It doesn't have to cost a lot—give your friend a thoughtful offering of thanks.

At the end of this transaction we want "everyone's integrity to remain intact," Cox said. "That's how we want this to end up, especially with friends. Integrity is doing what you say that you will do."

Seize this as an opportunity to negotiate a deal in a safe place with your friend. This kind of exchange can build your business acumen and strengthen your relational bond with your friend.

SOME FINAL THOUGHTS

The difference between a gift and a loan is that a gift isn't meant to be returned. So, if you give money to a friend, or your friend gives you money, it's an offering rather than an investment. An investment—even when loaned lovingly—is when you expect something in return.

And, of course, these days many people are crowd-sourcing as a way of gathering needed funds—everything from paying medical bills and rent to financing creative projects, such as opening a restaurant or producing a travel blog. A friend of mine spoke about this recently, saying, "I like the fact that as a society, we are creating ways to help our friends out collectively, which to me is a sign of hope."

I've been humbled by the generosity of many friends throughout my life. Unfortunately, I have lost contact with a lot of these people. So, I pay it forward, which means that I give money anonymously (when I can) to someone in my friend network who needs financial help. This way there's no ego, no debt, and no expectations for future gifts. It's as if I'm honoring my past friends by supporting my current ones.

Being smarter about money, loans, and gifts is often about changing our minds, becoming more generous and creative when sharing with friends, and savvier about our own resources.

And since many of the financial issues that come up involve life changes of some kind, that's what we'll look at next: going through the big transitions.

Transitions I

When Big Life Changes Blow In

*L*et's face it, we don't usually relish going through big transitions in our lives, especially those not of our own doing. And why would we? There's a lot of stress around being fired or laid off at work, divorcing, facing illness or the death of someone we love. And even those major shifts we feel are positive or asked for, such as starting college, changing careers, marrying, becoming pregnant, or retiring—involve a lot of stress.

So, it's likely that when we're going through a big life change, we can easily lose sight of how we're behaving toward our friends. My friend Nora recently reminded me of a time more than a decade ago when she found me to be a real pain in the butt. "You were hard to be around," Nora said. "Negative, often complaining. And whatever I suggested, you'd get defensive. Or wouldn't listen."

I knew exactly what she was talking about. I don't remember this time fondly either, because within the space of two months my rent went up, my roommate moved out, a work project fell through, and my car broke down. All at once, I had to find a new place to live, move into it, fix my car, reestablish my work, and bolster my bank account. I felt besieged by what was going on. I was so focused on myself—*me, me, me!*—that I ended up alienating some of my friends. Nora stuck it out, but one couple in particular didn't. This was Malia and Cliff, who were my landlords at the time.

I'd become good friends with them during my six-year tenancy. Then, when I went by to say my goodbyes and pick up my security deposit, Malia told me they'd be keeping $600.00 of that deposit for a cleaning fee.

"Cleaning fee!" I was incredulous. "I spent the whole week cleaning!"

"You didn't wash the windows," Malia said.

"Wash the windows?" I was in a daze. I hadn't even thought about the windows. "Why are you telling me this now, when I can't do anything about it?" Had they purposefully withheld this information from me?

"I thought you knew," was all Malia said, and right then there was no point arguing with her.

From my perspective, the issue was that I *needed* that $600.00! I gave these friends some empty air-kisses, but I was so upset, I could barely say goodbye.

Now I know. It didn't have to happen this way.

IN TIMES OF CHANGE

During our own times of stress, we're juggling so much that it's easy to lose sight of the big picture—the larger perspective that includes our friendships.

And when one of our friends is going through a major transition, we may need to give them more tender loving care. I go into this later in the chapter.

For right now, let's start with what we can do to keep friendships when we're the ones in transition. For instance, it's helpful to consider that when you're stressed, you may be the one who isn't returning phone calls. You may be so worried, so busy with your survival questions—*Where am I going to live? What am I going to do now that my spouse has left me? How can I find a new job?*—that you don't even think about how you're treating the people around you. "Grumpy/frumpy" is the description University of Arkansas psychology professor Scott H. Eidelman has for people going through these kinds of transitions—even though, he told me, they don't see themselves this way at all. "I'm not sure if the person going through the transition is necessarily aware that they're treating others differently," Eidelman added.[1]

The short of it is that when we're under stress, we have less time and energy to give to others—yet we want our friends to show up for us! I've certainly spent time sitting in an empty apartment, feeling vulnerable and lonely as I waited for a furniture van to arrive, crying and asking myself, *Why on earth did I move cross country?* It's OK to vent like this, either alone or with others, but at some point in the arc of a transition it's necessary to engage your brain to figure out options and strategies. This is where your close friends are invaluable. They're the ones who can offer clear options on how to move forward, who can keep you focused on the next step.

Your friends can do this, however, *only if you reach out to them*! And this reaching out is eminently worthwhile because these friends are not experiencing turmoil over your situation in the way you are and so they are more likely to have a clearer perspective. There is one other advantage to reaching out to friends when you're troubled—if you do, they'll be more likely to reach out to you when they're going through a tough time.

And making transitions *is hard for everyone.* This is a topic Eidelman looked into in his study: *The longer something is thought to exist, the better it is thought to be.*[2] This is why it's often difficult for people to make changes—and why we get stuck in habits. Eidelman pointed out that most of us are pretty averse to change. "We prefer what we're familiar with," he said, "because we'd rather stick with something that's good enough than to take a chance and roll the dice." And possibly lose everything. When our lives are in transition, we have moved out of a situation where we can coast on automatic and into a spot where we have to evaluate our actions and take more risks. In other words, we have to think. And thinking constantly is challenging—for most of us, exhausting.

How can we help our friends face change?

"I have two ideas that come to mind that I think could make a difference," Eidelman said. "First, give people an extra dose of comfort. Then they're going to be more willing to step out of their comfort zone." Invite a friend facing change over for a really relaxing lunch; send them their favorite flowers; take them on a walk in nature. . . . About the time I had to leave my apartment, a friend of mine invited me to housesit, so I went from an apartment to a whole house, and that house was in a quiet suburb within commuting distance to LA. It was just what I needed at the time. That's comfort.

Eidelman's second idea for aiding a friend to deal with change is to help them see that this change was inevitable. "People have an amazing capacity to rationalize," Eidelman said, "and if they think something's going to happen, they'll find a way to justify it so that it may actually be a good thing." This makes the big transition and all of the changes it brings a lot less daunting.

Change is, of course, a part of life. There are lots of ways it can come at us. Let's look at some of these specifically—beginning with what happened to two friends when one of them got married. This is a real-life story.

Marriage

Sara and Edie had been best friends from the ninth grade on—shared family secrets, one purple dress, and even the occasional lover. At some point after college, Edie met the man of her life just as Sara was coming off a bad romance. For the first time, Sara was aware that she and her best friend were on different wavelengths. When she heard that Edie was planning a wedding, Sara said, "It kind of blew my mind. Edie and I hadn't ever talked about our getting married. It wasn't a big interest of mine, and to my knowledge it wasn't a big interest to her—which is why I was pretty surprised."

It was after the wedding that problems came. Every time Sara wanted to hang out with Edie, Edie's husband was there. And Edie kept bringing up the idea of marriage to Sara. Finally, Sara recalled, they had "a terrible, terrible fight," and for a long time, they stopped talking. It seemed that Edie had gone into another phase of life and couldn't bring along her old buddy—or felt she couldn't—unless her buddy went into this new phase as well.

This is not an unusual outcome when one friend marries and another doesn't. I've heard my single friends say they feel they're being treated like a third wheel by their married friends. Sometimes they feel they have less social status because they're flying solo, and sometimes it's just that their married friends think it's important to balance the numbers at a dinner party. "It's like the world out there is an ark," was Sara's take on this. "Like people have to go on two by two."

Three years after her fight with Edie, Sara was married and expecting her first child. With this pregnancy, Sara figured that her old friend would once again take her "back into the fold." Initially, she was rebellious and resistant. It rankled her to be accepted for doing what was conventional.

But friendship is friendship, and so Sara decided to examine her resistance. She said, "I realized friends go into a tunnel when they get married, because I've seen so many people do it." Sara decided that, through a mutual friend, she would let Edie know about the pregnancy. "Then if she made an overture, or a gesture, to connect, I would do my best to be open." Edie did take that step and, in Sara's words, "It was a slow, cautious reconnection, but it's fully healed now."

For Sara, her close friend bonds can be as strong as marriage commitments. "I'm in it with both feet," she said, "and sometimes it'll be messy."

Sara and I spoke about how we have that kind of friendship, and then our conversation drifted from marriage into divorce. Almost as a caveat, Sara said that if John and I ever divorced, she'd maintain a friendship with both of us. She and I bantered for a few minutes about how, in this new relational world we live in, there can be a question of "who gets the friends after the divorce?"

What it comes down to is this: getting out of a marriage can be just as challenging for friendship as getting into one.

Divorce

Amelia and her husband, Ben, used to get together with two other couples. They'd go to each other's homes on Friday nights for cards or a movie. I joined them all once as a surprise guest at Amelia's big fortieth birthday bash, a gift Ben arranged for her. Amelia was an old friend, but we lived in different cities and hadn't seen much of each other recently. That night as she laughed and chatted with her guests, I felt like I was watching her act in a play—as if she wasn't really enjoying her own party. After everyone had left and Ben had gone to bed, Amelia and I talked late into the night about what was really going on. Ben worked until all hours and on weekends, showed up late to family events—or didn't show up at all.

So, three months later it was no surprise when she called to say she'd left Ben. It seems, however, that the other couples they hung out with *were* surprised. One of the wives made a special trip to convince Amelia to stay with Ben. Amelia told her, "He's a lovely man, he's a good father, but we're not meant to be together." This woman evidently went home angry because she never returned Amelia's calls—and never included her in an invitation again. The whole group cut Amelia off. After the divorce they all sided with Ben and dropped her.

This shocked Amelia, and that's why she wanted me to put her story in the book: "When people divorce, other people side." It had never occurred to her that by leaving Ben—a huge life transition—she was also going to lose the people she had seen as her closest friends.

So I asked Amelia why these friends were so shocked, because most of the time, it would be our friends who'd notice, or at least suspect, a pending divorce. "They were definitely Team Ben from the get-go," Amelia said. "They were *his* friends, and I integrated with them. I thought at the time that these were my essential friends. Now I look back and see that they were fake friends. And I was fake too, always putting on the happy face: everything's perfect." It's what Amelia now calls putting on the "Barbie and Ken show" for everybody.

This group traveled together, ate together, drank together—a fun-loving, Facebook kind of life.

"There were times in the marriage," Amelia said, "when I would cry in the shower because I felt so alone. The moments when I was physically alone were very hard. Then I'd put on my big girl pants and my makeup and put on *that* smile."

Everyone has their breaking point, and Amelia's arrived when her husband went on a ten-day business trip. "I had all that time to myself, wallowing in alcohol to try to ease the pain. Then I'd sober up and tell myself, *this is not working!*" She built up the nerve to talk it over with Ben. Then, as soon as he arrived home after his trip, she asked for a divorce. He was shocked.

The only people who weren't surprised were her parents. Of course, her mother and father knew Amelia like her husband and his friends never had.

After that, she would hang out with a work friend, a shoe rep, who Amelia knew through her job as a shoe shop manager. "I got very close to her," Amelia said, "We'd always do Vegas together, going to all the shoe conventions." And that friend let Amelia stay at her house for a time, during the divorce.

Other than that, Amelia didn't have many friends at the beginning of this difficult time of transition. She reached out to some of her older friends—"people I hadn't paid a lot of attention to in a long time," she said. "They turned out to be better friends than my current 'friends' in the circle that abandoned me. . . . I lost the whole pack I'd spent so many years with. It was a very lonely, very sad time. I didn't just lose my husband; I lost everything."

Amelia is not the only person this has happened to. Couples like having couples for friends, according to a study conducted by two professors from the University of Maryland School of Social Work, Geoffrey L. Greif and Kathleen Holtz Deal. Out of a sample of 123 couples and 58 divorcees, about two-thirds had friendships with couples that split up. When this happens, Greif writes in an article, "Over half said that the friendship ended with one person [in the couple], and one in eight said it ended with both; in about one-third both friendships were reportedly maintained."[3]

Greif names some of the reasons it can be difficult for those who are married to maintain friendships with either one or both of a newly separated couple: not wanting to take sides, feeling uncomfortable as a couple around the new singles. Greif adds that sometimes the couple's "own relationship is threatened when their friends break up."

I find it interesting that both of the other couples who hung out with Amelia and Ben later divorced. And, ironically, Amelia continued a friendship with her ex-husband, Ben, and his second wife—even after their children were grown!

Greif writes that for those who were divorced, "almost four in ten said that they lost all couple friendships and almost two in ten said they lost some couple friendships with the divorce."

There was, however, one other statistic he mentions, which I found fascinating: individual (read "single") friends—that is, friends to one or the other in the divorcing pair—"were more apt to stick with the divorcing people (60.3 percent of the divorced indicated this) and one in six said they became closer with their individual friends."

To me, this statistic shows just how vital it is for couples to have single friends in their lives. These are the people who are more likely to hang around if the marriage breaks down! Having been single for most of my adult life, I've always been comfortable having couple friends when flying solo, and single friends now that I'm married. It's about finding balance in your network of close friends. And when a couple you're friendly with gets a divorce, you might decide to find ways, even if separately, to include them both in your life—that is, if you like them both.

Greif suggests some ways to approach this conversation:

- If your friends are divorcing: *We would like to continue our friendship and do not want to have to choose sides.*
- If you are divorcing: *Even though we are splitting up, I would like to maintain our friendship and will try to not have you choose sides.*
- From either perspective: *Let's continue to make this a work in progress because I value you in my (our) life.*

In his writing, Greif also notes something I point out in chapter 1: people who have friends lead healthier and longer lives than those who don't. So, embracing and preserving these loving bonds is vital.

HOW TO SHOW UP FOR A FRIEND IN TRANSITION

It is important to show up for your friends who are going through life changes—and I want to be clear about what showing up *truly* means. You can turn up with casseroles, drive friends around town, listen to them, or, if you choose, give them cash—but it doesn't mean squat if these actions aren't offered with caring, kindness, and love.

Once when I had just been laid off from a terrific, high-paying job I had made a cross-country relocation for, I felt vulnerable and confused. To cheer me up, a friend offered to make me dinner. As soon as I arrived at her place, she insisted I look at her fun photos from a recent holiday. The phone rang, and I heard her say to the person on the other end, "No, I can't come over tonight. Someone's here." She sighed. "She just got dumped by her boss, and I guess she needed someone to complain to."

I froze. Had she really said that? Wow, it stung! When she got off the phone, I called her out on it. She apologized because, of course, she saw how her behavior had upset me.

We talked this through in depth that night, and, ultimately, she saw that her lack of empathy was a deeply rooted trait from her childhood. As it happened, talking this through did bring us to a better place with each other, turning a potentially uncomfortable evening into something more cheerful. To me, these are the moments of opportunity in life, when we can shift the energy with a friend from hurt to greater understanding.

Caring for friends who are dealing with turmoil in their lives may be intuitive for some, but many of us find it difficult to know what to say in the face of life changes. I believe this skill can be learned.

Here are some ways you can show up for a friend in transition:

1. If you hear your friend has been laid off or fired, call the person and say something like this: *Hi, I heard the news. If there's anything I can do, please let me know.*
2. Empathize by listening, and offer them a time to chat in person: *If you're around Saturday, do you want to grab lunch?* When you meet, allow them to talk about how they feel, and if they get emotional, let them vent.
3. Find out what their needs are right now, and offer to help: *Can I give you a lift to the airport?* Or, *do you need time to do errands? I can babysit your kids Saturday morning.*
4. When you offer to help, be specific: *OK, so I'll be there at 10:00 a.m. to babysit, and you said you'll be back around 1:00 p.m., right?* When a person is overwhelmed, details tend to slip through the cracks. Whenever I'm upset, I often end up locking my keys

in the car or myself out of the house. You need to be clear on behalf of you both.

5. Sometimes you may need to be assertive. I remember my sister telling me that after she'd retired, she went into a slump. She stopped answering calls, her hair was a knotty mess, and she didn't get out of her dressing gown until noon (trust me, this is a huge anomaly for her). One day, she heard a knock at the door and opened it to find a dear friend was standing on her doorstep. The friend was worried because she hadn't heard from my sister. She looked my sister up and down and said, "Come on, we're going to get your hair done. We'll figure out the rest later." Believe it or not, this was the trigger that got my sister back to her old fabulous self!

6. Assist in problem solving, or brainstorming, once the emotion has calmed down and your friend realizes it's time to focus on the future. Let them take the lead and build on their ideas—such as, *I know you're looking for a place to live, but why don't you stay and work from our place for the summer?* Or, more simply, *If you like, I'd be happy to edit your résumé for you.*

7. It may be necessary to pay attention to a friend's obsessive behavior. A close friend became obsessed with her ex-boyfriend's new life and would troll his Facebook page for hours. So, we put her on a Facebook diet. At first, she could only look at his page once a day. Then, when she managed that, we shifted it to three times a week. Eventually, we got it down to once a week, until it petered out. So, you can establish constructive, creative solutions as well.

BUILD ON THE POSITIVE

In the twenty-first century we can shape our experiences in new ways. We have more information about our brain and our emotions—our personal operating system, so to speak. And this information can guide us to taking new stances—such as turning a bad experience with a friend into an exploration—into another experience entirely! It's one of the reasons I wrote this book, and in the process of writing it, I saw this verified again and again—in my own life!

One of the "truths" I'd observed for years is that when one thing goes wrong in life, many other things tend to fall apart as well. I was reading a book, *Switch: How to Change Things When Change Is Hard*, in which two academics discuss new ways to assess challenging situations. One of the examples they gave hit home for me big time.

The hypothetical goes like this: if you're a parent and your teenager comes home with a report card that has a mix of As, Bs, and an F, where do you put your attention? You're likely to focus on the F, right? That F becomes your preoccupation. What the book's authors and the creator of this very example—management trainer Marcus Buckingham—suggest is that it's important for us to step away from this kind of thinking. We need to focus on the As. It's the As that give us a foundation upon which we can build.[4]

Focus on the As! What a revelation! Remember how I lost that $600.00 to my former landlords and one-time friends, Malia and Cliff? Reading this simple suggestion, I realized how I had allowed one unhappy business transaction with Malia and Cliff to define a six-year friendship. Our financial dispute, followed by my air-kiss and my flee into oblivion, had been my image of these lovely friends for the past twelve years.

Talking this over with my husband, I began to list all of the As in my friendship with Malia and Cliff. Like the time Cliff helped me with a screenplay I was writing and introduced me to an agent. Once, Malia and Cliff had asked if I'd like to join them on a vacation to a tropical island. This didn't work out, but what a sweet gesture! And Malia had spoken with me about a beautiful experience she had with her meditation teacher, who'd suggested to Malia that she make everyone her friend—which was my inspiration for this book.

So, our friendship had a lot of As. And that's when I decided to find these friends again.

This wasn't especially easy. More than twelve years had gone by, and these people had no social media presence whatsoever. After scrambling around the internet for hours, however, I found that my old address was on a real estate page and that Malia and Cliff were having an estate sale that very day! How's that for timing!

I found an old, tattered address book in my filing cabinet, with a phone number for them. I called, and an electronic voice asked me to leave a message—which I did, even though it was anyone's guess whether this was still their number. But it was, and a few hours later Malia called back. They'd been at the beach to avoid all the foot traffic during the estate sale. She and I talked nonstop for forty-five minutes, just catching up—their selling everything and moving to Hawaii with "only a few suitcases," and my recent marriage to John.

"Next time you're in town, give us a call," Malia said. "We'd love to see you again and meet John!"

A few weeks later, the four of us were sitting on their back porch, looking at their tropical garden and drinking Southern-style tea (lots of sugar, lots of ice). It had been twelve years, and we'd all moved into different kinds of lives. "Has Hollywood changed?" Cliff asked me, "or did we just become older and unwilling to deal with it anymore?"

I laughed, "Probably a bit of both."

Being back with the two of them, chatting about how life was going, it just didn't seem important to go over what happened those many years ago. We had all moved on.

As John and I drove away that afternoon, he said that what amazed him was their describing me as the one friend they'd made out of all their other tenants. It had surprised me too, but then, it had been so very easy to drop back into each other's lives—once I'd been willing to focus on the As.

The transitions we discussed in this chapter, while often difficult and sometimes even heartbreaking, are not what you'd consider life-threatening. In the next chapter, however, we look at these more serious changes, such as a critical illness—the kind that can leave you fighting for your life. And this specialized topic needed its own chapter.

· 8 ·

Transitions II

When Illness Strikes

$\mathcal{W}$hen I was in my mid-twenties, a friend—I'd say she was a close social friend—found out she had a cancerous tumor in her abdomen. Layla and I were both expat Aussies living in Santa Barbara, and we enjoyed each other's company at parties, the occasional book club meeting, or for a cup of tea. At times she had troubles with her long-term boyfriend and complained about him to me—especially at the end of their relationship, when he fell in love with a woman from Spain. Then Layla got cancer, and because she had no money to speak of or family nearby, suddenly I became her only support system.

I felt overwhelmed. Layla and I didn't have a long history together. Now I was spending hours visiting her in the hospital, and once she was discharged, she moved in with me. One morning, trying to be casual, I asked how long she thought she'd be staying. She looked deeply hurt and began to cry. Through her sobs, she said, "I don't have anywhere else to go. Can't I just stay here for a while? You're my friend."

I told her she could stay as long as she liked. What else could I say? I felt terrible.

But probably not as terrible as she felt at the time.

Looking back, I can see that I dishonored Layla *and* myself. I did step forward, but I wasn't really there. By "there," I mean fully present in the situation and to my own on-the-ground, in-the-moment responses. If I had been, this could have been a huge lesson for me: an opportunity to learn about how to accept greater responsibility and how to navigate a difficult time with grace. Instead, for the two weeks that Layla stayed with me, I felt burdened by what was happening and, I suspect, scared by her illness and the sense that I was taking on more than I could handle. I didn't know what to do, and at the time, I didn't consciously perceive what I was feeling. Looking back, I can see that I was uncomfortable, maybe even a little resentful. And, of course, until the end, I didn't know this was going to be for just two weeks. It felt frighteningly open-ended.

I'm probably not the only one who has struggled to be fully present, or show up at all, when a friend faces a life-threatening illness. And I'm certainly not the only one who wishes in retrospect that they had acted with greater consciousness at the time. But through the years I have learned how to be a better communicator—demonstrating my concern, asking the other person what *they* need from me—even when I may feel uneasy about navigating this difficult terrain, which includes their fears and my fears for them, as well as the confusion and uncertainty we both may have.

After decades of self-inquiry, I see this as a friendship opportunity missed. Now, I try *not* to miss an opportunity. With this in mind, I start this chapter by discussing the importance of cultivating compassion. I feel that it's important to spend a moment considering this before we get to the tensions and conflicts that can arise; these come up later in the chapter.

To start with, it's important to pinpoint what *compassion* is and how it differs from *empathy* and *sympathy*. To feel *empathy* is to be aware of another person's thoughts, feelings, or experience. In fact, we can feel empathy simply watching a funny or sad character in a movie—that's our mirror neurons at work. *Sympathy*, on the other hand, involves a cognitive understanding that the experience another person is having is painful. This is why, for instance, you send a friend a sympathy card after her father's death. Both empathy and sympathy are components of compassion, but they are not the whole description. With true compassion, "you feel the pain of another (i.e., empathy), or you recognize that the person is in pain (i.e., sympathy), and then you do your best to alleviate the person's suffering from that situation."[1] So, compassion involves taking action.

Acting on our compassion is how we, as a species, have survived. Most of us have heard about Charles Darwin's research on "survival of the fittest"—a phrase that was *not* coined by Darwin. In fact, UC Berkeley psychology professor Dacher Keltner claims that Darwin's theories are more aligned to a "survival of the kindest."[2] In his own writing, Darwin argues that our instincts are not hardwired to be selfish; we're hardwired to be sympathetic and kind.[3] If we cooperate as individuals, our communities are more likely to flourish, and the more our communities flourish, the more likely we are to raise healthy offspring—the essential component for evolution.

Even though compassion is a component of a thriving community, it is not an automatic response. In observing myself and others, I've seen that compassion is like a muscle that must be strengthened through use.

For example, a friend once asked me to drive her husband to a medical center for his first chemo treatment after a cancer operation. While I was more than happy to help, I suggested to her that he'd probably be more comforted if she was there, rather than me.

"But I have to go to work," she said.

"Take a sick day," I told her. "Your husband's sick, and he'd love your support. Your bosses will probably understand."

She thought about this for a moment, and then she smiled. "Yes. Yes, of course. That's a great idea!"

Apparently, it was. A year later, I found that this same friend, having seen what her presence did to support her husband, took time off to help a friend who was in the hospital with cancer. She had activated her compassion.

Now here's a story from the perspective of the person receiving compassion, a close friend who faced a life-threatening illness more than a decade ago. This woman, Jessica, had been out of touch with her family for years; it was her friends who supported her—some staying with her for the long haul while others helped her as best they could in the short term. These life events appear to separate the essential friends (the long haul) from the collaborators (fulfilling more immediate emotional interests and needs).

The irony for me is that even though Jessica and I weren't close during her illness—at the time I didn't even know she was sick—our friendship blossomed because of it. This happened toward the end of her ordeal.

I feel that the story of her illness is worth telling in some detail.

ACTIVATING COMPASSION

Jessica's medical drama began during the Christmas season, her favorite time of year. She'd been looking forward to heading out to many festive parties with friends and her media clients—at the time Jessica was an entertainment consultant. On this particular year, however, she had to cancel all her invitations because she'd caught a cold, which turned into a flu—a bad flu that she couldn't seem to shake. On the morning of her third doctor's appointment, she felt too exhausted to stand by the sink to brush her hair. She had to lie down on the damp mat on the bathroom floor, awkwardly trying to blow-dry her hair. And that's when Jessica knew something was terribly wrong.

She can't remember how she drove herself to the doctor's office. When she walked into the reception area, the nurse took one look at her and gasped. "You're as yellow as a banana," the nurse told her. "You're going to sit in this wheelchair, and we're taking you around the corner to the ER."

Jessica arrived at the hospital's emergency room with a 106-degree fever. She made a crucial call to a client from her hospital gurney and then passed out. A few days later, the doctors told Jessica that she had Hodgkin's lymphoma, cancer of the blood. As Jessica recalled later, they told her in a very matter-of-fact way, "We're starting chemo. Your hair's going to fall out, and you're going to throw up. We're getting started right away."

She said, "OK."

Within a few days, her friends and clients started showing up to see her. In this early stage of Jessica's illness, her visitors wore face masks and stood in semi-darkness. The only light in the room was the eerie neon glow from those machines because the staff kept the overheads off and the blinds down. Jessica could only make out people's silhouettes.

There was one friend, however, who was noticeably absent. Through a twist of fate, Ellen, Jessica's most loving confidante and closest friend for twenty years, was recovering from breast cancer at the time, going through her own chemo treatments in San Francisco, where she lived. Even so, the two of them talked regularly by phone.

Many other supportive people were around, however, to help Jessica. They ran errands for her, brought her mail to the hospital, and made sure she had clean nighties. One friend arrived with a soft, comfy dressing gown and a stacked deli sandwich—sliced turkey on pumpernickel, Jessica's absolute favorite food. A client sent Jessica a small box of pears, and even though her eating wasn't back to normal, this box of ripe fruit lifted her spirits.

During this time, Jessica's friend Paige became the substitute for a "family" member—her intrepid advocate. She stood by Jessica's hospital bed for hours, listening to the whirring machines somewhere in the background, committed to being there for Jessica through this whole ordeal. This included meeting the whole cast of characters, such as Jessica's doctors and nurses who, with Jessica's permission, invited Paige into their medical discussions. "I would ask questions to try to understand," Paige told me. "Once they were trying to tape on the IV, and Jessica had a really bad reaction to this blue tape they were using. She's very sensitive. I remember telling them, 'No, no, no!'"

Paige had met Jessica seven years before in a professional setting, in television. At the time, Paige was a production assistant, a go-getter backstage, organizing and helping everyone—even though she wanted to try her hand at on-air hosting. One broadcast day, when Jessica was in the studio's greenroom with a client, someone pointed her out to Paige. "That woman could be helpful to you," Paige's friend told her. "She used to work for a big talent agency, and now she's going out on her own."

Paige introduced herself to Jessica, and they felt an instant connection. They met for coffee, then started going to church together and to industry networking events. Jessica gave Paige tangible support to move in the professional direction she wanted. This helped Paige land an on-air reporter job in Texas. Paige saw Jessica as a big sister, which made it natural for her to step in and help when Jessica became ill.

At the time, Paige had work, but nothing pressing. "I wasn't working a gazillion hours on a talk show," she said. "I wasn't a reporter running around with my hair on fire. I could actually stop and put my toe in her shoe"—which was a lovely way of saying that she could be fully present for Jessica. She didn't have the kind of family or career constraints that many of Jessica's other friends had at the time.

I asked Paige how she managed to stand for all those hours in semi-darkness, watching Jessica sleep.

"I have a friend I've known since fifth grade," Paige said. "Her name's Natalie. She's the most peaceful person. I always brought her to mind. I'd think, *What would Natalie do? Natalie would just be here. Natalie would offer comfort and hold Jessica's hand and let her know she's going to be OK.*"

So, that's what Paige did, and after a while, it started to feel more comfortable for her. "I started to feel like this is part of who I am."

Isn't that interesting! Expressing behavior that she admired in someone else made that behavior natural for Paige as well. By holding Jessica's hand, Paige became the kind of person who would offer comfort to a friend by holding the friend's hand. We often underestimate the power in simply holding a friend's hand. In one of his studies, Keltner looks at the effect human touch has on our sense of well-being: "Friendly touch stimulates activation in the vagus nerve, a bundle of nerves in the chest that calms fight-or-flight cardiovascular response and triggers the release of oxytocin, which enables feelings of trust."[4]

This is in sync with a study in which a psychologist and medical doctor look at how acts of compassion confer positive health benefits on the one showing the compassion. I discuss this study later in the chapter.

WHAT IS TRULY HELPFUL?

Although Jessica didn't remember all her friends in this way, some were not especially helpful, even when they thought they were. Jessica told me quite a bit about the unsought medical advice she received from some of her friends. One of her good friends, Fiona, was a medical tech who would stand by Jessica's bed on her visits and, in Jessica's words, "It was just '*blah-blah-blah.*' She was very verbose about what I needed."

The last thing Jessica wanted from Fiona—or anyone else for that matter—was information about healing diets and alternative treatments and exciting new therapies being explored in Mexico. One day Jessica interrupted one of these conversations happening at her hospital bedside, saying, "You know what, guys, that's great. Thank you. I don't want to be disrespectful, but I'm about to die right now. I have a diagnosis, and I can't go somewhere for a week and think about it."

Just imagine the energy it took for Jessica in that moment, lying in her hospital bed, to break into the discussion that was coming at her! Just imagine how all of this sounded to her—a woman who had neither time nor energy nor, truth be told, *money* to explore these far-flung, exotic options.

"And she never came once and truly helped me," Jessica said.

In another example of less-than-helpful support, Jessica's then boyfriend had a phobia of hospitals, so instead of visiting her there, he spent the time while she was hospitalized painting her apartment. He had wanted to surprise her, and he did—but it wasn't a wholly successful gift. Even though she was grateful for her freshly painted apartment— "Everything looked so nice!"—it turned out that the smell of new paint was not the best welcome-home from a sterile hospital environment. He had meant well, but the fumes made Jessica nauseated and headachy.

The person who responded with what Jessica truly needed at this time was Ellen, the friend who had been through cancer therapy herself. Once Ellen finished her own chemotherapy, she flew to LA to spend a week with Jessica to support her during hers. Ellen *knew* what was needed. Jessica noticed that instead of asking her, "Would you *like* a cup of tea?" Ellen would ask her, "*Can you have* a cup of tea?" In other words, Ellen understood what Jessica's physical constraints were. So, she was able to word her questions to make it clear she understood, and truly listened to, what Jessica had to say.

During this time the two of them would laugh and talk about many topics—from wig styles to why it's best not to get a manicure. ("Because," as Jessica explained, "you can't do anything that will poke your skin.") Receiving this kind of information from a beloved friend who had recently been on the same road herself was invaluable to Jessica.

And, if you're the friend offering help, it's important to be compassionate with yourself as well. There are friends who can ask more of us than we are truly able to give in this circumstance. You need to check in with yourself to see how much you feel comfortable offering, and then being more aware about setting (necessary!) boundaries. It's up to you to set these boundaries. I realize that setting boundaries is often difficult between friends, in any number of circumstances, not just illness, which is why I discuss boundaries in more detail in the next chapter. The baseline here is to take your own needs into consideration when helping a friend.

And, of course, there are friends who can ask more of us than we are truly able to give in their circumstances. There are also friends who may sink deeper and deeper into physical illness. Or into mental illness. Or even into addiction. These friends seem to need more, much more, than we're capable of giving them. Once you have offered as much as you can—you might think of this as hitting a wall—then give yourself permission to step aside, at least for now. And trust that this is the best thing for you to do.

This is what some of Jessica's friends eventually did: they stepped aside.

FRIENDSHIP LIMITS

Jessica recognized that there was a toll on a number of her friends—especially the people she had known primarily through work, her collaborator friends. By the time she was getting better, many of these people had drifted away, out of her life.

We've all probably experienced this. You or your friend have a huge life-altering experience, and once it's over there's not much left to offer each other. Like my relationship with Layla, whom I talked about at the beginning of this chapter. After Layla returned home to Australia, we didn't stay in contact. I think of this as friend burnout. Or perhaps she felt that I hadn't been there for her when she needed me most.

This can arise in a situation where one friend is asking a lot of the other—whether this is the result of a financial setback, a divorce, or, as in this case, a serious illness.

Talking about a friend's illness probably makes you feel like a bystander, which can be uncomfortable or even daunting. We may not *want* to talk about the illness. Yet it is *important* to talk about the illness—as long as we're careful not to offer unwelcome advice—because the illness is a huge factor in your friend's life and to not talk about it is to ignore what's happening—the elephant in the room, so to speak.

And let's face it, the fallout from a serious illness doesn't necessarily stop once the person gets better. In Jessica's case, after surviving her illness, she faced whopping medical bills. "I had to file bankruptcy because of the bills," she said. "That's an element we haven't really touched on. People were helping me financially because I couldn't work. I had health insurance, and then I get the letter—in July, I think it was. I had just turned forty in March. So suddenly in July my insurance was going up to $750 or $800 a month." Before that time, she'd paid less than half that amount, and this leap in payments was something she simply couldn't manage.

Many people live in countries that have a robust health system, and for now the United States has what has been called "affordable care." That could, however, change at any time, depending on the political climate. So, even though it's less likely in these days that an illness would bankrupt a person in the United States, other costs can mount in an alarming way. So, at what point, as a friend, do you say *enough is enough*? For issues around money, it's probably worth going back to review the financial protocols I've set up in chapter 6. These may help you decide what you are able, or willing, to offer a friend.

From the point of view of the person who has gone through the illness, there are other, even more significant shifts that can occur, and these are not always predictable. "I think that most people assume that when you have a near-death experience, or cancer, you have a wake-up call," Jessica said. "The way I see it is that an illness like this exhausts you. Afterward, you know your limits in a new way. I did a lot of thinking about the *before* and the *after*, because this illness punctuated my life in so many significant ways."

She realized that now she wasn't very good at dealing with emotional stress. This meant Jessica couldn't return to her high-pressure career in entertainment. And *this* meant she was no longer in show business—and is probably why several of her collaborator friends dropped out of her life. Jessica and these people no longer had their work in common, and, as well, they were now operating at different financial levels. Jessica had to start to live on a budget. There was one dear friend, for instance, with whom Jessica used to love shopping and going out to dinner, but that friend eventually stopped calling so much. They still go on the occasional beach walk together, something that Jessica enjoys. Although these people, and others, dropped out of her life, and Jessica no longer had the energy to keep all these relationships active.

So, now, I want to bring it back to the earlier discussion about compassion. We can easily see how compassion helps its recipient, and we've spoken about how it helps a whole community, but what we may consider a golden virtue is as helpful to the person who gives it. And that's hard science talking.

THE HEALTH BENEFITS OF COMPASSION

In one study I read, a pair of academics set out to compare two different types of happiness. These are *hedonic* (which is an immediate response from a sensory experience such as eating tasty food, watching a beautiful sunset, or laughing with a friend) and *eudaemonic* (where most of the sense of pleasure is derived from making a contribution to someone else, or a community or cause, or a beneficial discovery outside yourself).[5]

At a psychological self-reporting level, both of these forms of happiness registered high on the health and well-being metric. Yet in comparing the subjects' blood samples, the researchers found eudaemonic happiness to be associated with signs of better microbial health (low inflammation and high immune suppression) and hedonic happiness to be associated with the microbial reactions necessary for the flight-or-fight response of facing imminent danger (higher inflammation and lower immune suppression).[6] The latter response is necessary when we're ward-ing off a saber-toothed tiger or an enemy tribe—especially when we're alone—but if this flight-or-fight response is activated consistently, over the long term it is damaging to our health.[7]

So, is hedonic happiness actually bad for us? The two academics who conducted this research—Steve W. Cole from the David Geffen School of Medicine at UCLA and Barbara L. Fredrickson from the psychology department at the University of North Carolina at Chapel Hill—did not draw a conclusion so dire as that. In a lecture at Stanford University, Cole said it's fine to enjoy a good dinner or watch a beautiful sunset. He suggested, however, that we are healthier at the microbial level when we derive the bulk of our happiness from helping others or improving ourselves.[8] When the research subjects were operating in what Cole called "a compassionate mode," they were activating the parasympathetic nervous system, and this, he explained, actually inhibits the "fight-or-flight stress biology that's orchestrating these adverse gene expression profiles."[9]

I love the idea that the deeds done for the good of others have a healthy biological foundation. And there can be other unexpected benefits that emerge when we're helping others, such as making positive adjustments in our own life. I've seen this happen to myself and others. Paige gave a beautiful example of this when I asked her what she did while she was sitting in the waiting room during Jessica's chemo treatments.

"I'd journal a lot of times, and I would pray for Jessica," Paige said. "I'd ask for strength for her and for me." In praying for herself, Paige started questioning what she wanted from her own life. "I was at a real crossroads," she said, "trying to figure out where I was headed next." Around this same time, she and Jessica were having long, searching conversations. Jessica had always had a strong desire to travel, and it seems as if Paige had an unexpressed passion for travel that was ignited by these talks. "We ended up talking about my passion to go to see places that most people don't ever visit."

A month after Jessica's chemo ended, Paige traveled to Vietnam for a month. After that she went to Israel. "Talking with Jessica, I got in touch with a sense that life is short and that now was the time for me to do this." As Paige described it, helping Jessica was a springboard in her own life—an inspiration to do the things she most wanted to do.

Jessica said that she didn't find it surprising that her life-altering experience with illness shook up her friendships. "I was just happy to be alive," she said. And, naturally, this new stance altered the way she perceived her friends. Ironically, her experience paralleled my own life change, after my Big Shift birthday party—the party that launched this book. As Jessica put it, "I spent some time thinking about who I wanted to nurture in the next chapter of my story. Maybe, subconsciously, I knew that certain people would leave my life and that I needed to reach out to other people."

This is where I came in. I had known Jessica through work for about seven years, but we hadn't been in touch for a while—not uncommon in entertainment—and I didn't know she'd been ill. One day, out of the blue, she called to invite me to a cancer walk at a local city college. She told me she had just finished her chemo treatments. "I'd really like to get to know you better," she said, "And as this is something I'm doing right now. It would be nice if you could support me in it."

Of course, I said I'd be there.

Jessica and I reconnected on that blistering hot July day, and now, well over a decade later, we remain close friends—essential friends to each other. Jessica's instinct to reach out to me launched the next level of our beautiful friendship.

Boundaries

Set Them, Respect Them

Setting boundaries isn't easy—especially with friends. Why? They're our friends, and we love them, even when they're breaching some sort of protocol or trust. But often it's awkward, and even frustrating, to have to say something about this situation. We think, *Doesn't she know? How could she not know how I feel about this!* At times like these a boundary needs to be identified, put into words.

A friend had a situation like this with one of her close friends. When she was pregnant with her first child, Madelyn met Helen, who taught alternative child birthing classes. The two of them have been friends ever since, along with three other moms who attended those same classes. Because they raised their children together, they called themselves the Mothers. Madelyn adores Helen, describing her as "a really good-hearted person, smart, cultured, and a great movie critic!" (Madelyn loves movies.)

Yet Helen can also be pushy and, occasionally, demanding. Madelyn told me, "She's a person who, when she encounters a boundary, will keep at it until she gets what she wants." Even for the smaller arrangements, such as pushing to change the time or place of a dinner date the Mothers had planned together. They'd agree on six o'clock, then on that day Helen would want to change it to seven—she had a nail appointment, or some such activity. Initially, the others would accommodate her, but then it became a noticeable pattern—and this became annoying. They all had hectic work and personal lives, so the constant reshuffling threw off their own schedules.

"So, we established ground rules," Madelyn said. Even then, Helen still kept testing the waters. Madelyn can't remember who first set down the boundary, but it was clear: *From now on if a time and place is set, that's it—unless there's an emergency—and we hope to see you there.* And they all fell in line with this rule, no longer changing their plans to suit Helen. "Here's the time and place we're meeting. Hope you can make it." For a while, Helen kept testing them, but now she knows better—and even laughs about it.

Setting boundaries like this one, Madelyn said, is a matter of "figuring out what works for me." She added, "To be a good friend, you've got to get clear about who you are . . . to do some work on yourself."

Which is a key to this chapter. It's about knowing what you want in a friendship so when a friend crosses a line into territory that doesn't work for you, instead of dwelling on their behavior, you address the issue.

It's important for me to keep my close friend connections active, and this takes some effort on my part, a certain level of commitment and communication. And I have to admit that the amount of effort I put in corresponds to the level of friendship I have with that person, whether I see this person as an essential friend, a collaborator, or an associate.

Also, there are some people I would never think of as a friend at any level. These people transgress some kind of pre-friend boundary I have. For instance, if I perceive a person as mean spirited or a gossip, then I stay away. I know from experience that such a person would cause me emotional distress. Once, years ago, I was getting to know a well-traveled, witty woman who, just after meeting me, began telling tales about a mutual friend's private life. That was it for me. Done. Because if the mutual friend wanted me to know all of this, she would tell me herself. Also, I was quite aware that if this person was sharing another person's secrets, she'd soon be sharing mine.

So, let's get clarity on what setting a boundary with a friend means. It's when you take a stance about feeling resentment, frustration, or potential threat because of certain behavior. To do this, of course, you have to be clear—or become clear—about what your boundaries are in the first place.

Let me tell you about an old friend who used to give me "business leads." Craig would suggest I write a pitch or business proposal for this or that person—presumably for powerful friends of his. One of these guys, Craig told me, was running for mayor in a Californian town and could use some media training. I tried looking for this guy's online media presence but couldn't find him anywhere, which I thought was odd. Even so, I spent time researching the town and its demographics, and I wrote up a media training proposal—only to discover in a phone meeting that Craig set up for us that this man wasn't running for mayor at all but for the state legislature and didn't need or want my help! Craig had even misspelled his name!

I was really frustrated—and I took responsibility for it myself! This had happened several times before. I realized that I had never been clear with Craig that my time is money. So, in effect, I was giving my time to him at no cost. But not ever again!

The next time Craig pitched me a great idea on which I could lavish my time and energy, I said, "That sounds terrific! But before I get going, you need to raise $1,000 to pay me to write the proposal. Once I get that, I'll get started." Once I gave Craig a dollar amount and his own homework to do, guess what? Yep, he stopped calling me about pitching proposals to his "connections." I just needed to recognize this pattern and take a stand.

Some people need to hear boundaries vocalized, whereas others are able to pick up on more subtle signals. My thoughtful friends value my time. When I'm on a writing deadline, those who know me well won't call before three in the afternoon. They know that if they do, I will pick up the phone—because they know I *love* a distraction.

I try to do this myself. When I probe a friend about a particularly sensitive issue, if they abruptly change the subject, I back off. And unless this friend invites me back into that topic, I respectfully let it go.

I must admit that this hasn't always been the case for me. I have sometimes blundered through emotional turf I had no right to be in—and a friend has had to let me know (in no uncertain terms) that I crossed a line. Like the time I sent a guy a highly charged letter blaming him for his breakup with my brokenhearted friend. Like the time I attempted to matchmake for another friend at a professional networking event when she had neither asked for nor wanted my help. Needless to say, neither of these incidents ended happily—but, ultimately, I was grateful to be told, clearly, to back off.

On the other hand, when a friend has crossed that line with me, I, too, have been straightforward with that person.

At times, this straightforward approach to boundary setting has made people uncomfortable—and it's very likely the reason that person and I are no longer friends. This is what naturally happens when a connection is no longer thriving. And we really do want our friendships to thrive.

So, yes, it's possible to lose friends when setting boundaries. Yet I believe that for every level of friendship, whether new or old, it's perfectly acceptable—in fact, it's important—to set down boundaries if you feel a friend repeatedly crosses a line that upsets you by:

- being pushy or controlling,
- being thoughtless or inappropriate,
- being needy and uptight,
- making debilitating choices, or
- intruding on personal areas that don't concern them.

Speaking up about these issues is one way we let someone know what our rhythm is; it's how we share our likes and dislikes, our life views; it's how we demonstrate our character. It's why—as Timothy Levine, a professor of communication studies at the University of Alabama, pointed out to me—we are often more authentic with our friends than we are with our families and coworkers. With friends we feel we can be honest about who we are. If it doesn't work out, we can drop that person as a social contact; if it does, we have a life-enriching friendship. I go into more detail on this topic in chapter 10.

So, we've talked about how to address pushy or controlling friends—that's what was happening when Helen kept changing the agreements to suit herself and also what was happening with Craig, who was taking up my professional time without paying me. So, now, let's turn to the second on the list: being thoughtless and inappropriate.

OUT OF BOUNDS

Thoughtlessness comes in many packages, and making people wait for you is one that especially annoys me. One of my friends started to keep me waiting more and more often for both social events and business meetings. A few times we were supposed to meet at her apartment for a social date, yet she was nowhere to be found. On one of these times, she was doing her laundry and didn't have her phone with her. On another, I waited for her outside in my hot car while sending her text messages, and when she finally got back to me, she blamed me for not calling to confirm—a date we'd set up just a few days earlier! The day this woman rushed up flustered because she was late for a business meeting the two of us had with a third party, I said, "I'm just letting you know that in future I'm going to start the meeting on time, with or without you." Later, I told her I'd no longer wait more than fifteen minutes for her when we got together socially—a few minutes' grace is needed to figure in LA traffic. She got it, and recently told me that she's always on time to meetings and events now—thanks, in part, to our conversations.

Another boundary involves entering into a business or financial arrangement. The example I want to use here also involves Madelyn and Helen, but it took a lot more energy to resolve than finding a time and place to meet for dinner. Helen (the woman who liked to change plans) was told she'd have to move out of her rental apartment because it was being sold. She panicked. She had no savings for a security deposit on a new place; her main source of income was a small pension and a little business she'd been running on the side—out of that very apartment. Helen knew that Madelyn had an apartment that she rented out, and Helen asked if she could become the tenant. From Helen's perspective, this was simple math: she needed an apartment to rent, her friend had an apartment to rent. Easy peasy.

From Madelyn's perspective, she already had a terrific tenant—a man who paid his rent on time, had a solid job, fixed stuff in and out of the place, and was a dream to deal with. Madelyn saw no reason to put out this exemplary tenant—especially when she'd already had difficulty with Helen sticking to social agreements in their group, the Mothers.

So, even if Madelyn hadn't had that great tenant, she wouldn't have wanted to get entangled in a financial arrangement with a friend who was always negotiating, and then renegotiating.

This became quite challenging. Helen kept saying stuff like, "You have two homes; I have none"—guilt-tripping her friend.

And Madelyn did feel bad about Helen's plight. Yet she kept saying, "My answer is going to be no, and that's not going to change. I depend on that apartment for my income."

Madelyn admitted that setting this boundary wasn't easy. Throughout this process, Madelyn felt compelled to review her belief system "and really examine this situation." She didn't want to be cold-hearted. She came to the conclusion that her desire to be generous and philanthropic is congruent with setting this boundary with Helen. "I do love Helen," Madelyn said, "but it's about figuring out what works for me, too."

Doing business with friends is a huge topic, and the irony around this topic is that you may have a friend you adore talking with, hanging out with, going to the movies with—possibly an essential friend or a collaborator—yet you'd never loan this person cash or do business with them. And you may, on the other hand, have an associate friend whom you'd feel comfortable loaning money to or doing business with, yet would not choose to spend social time with.

For now, let's consider inappropriate behavior from our friends.

OVER-PERCEPTION BIAS

Some friends are both thoughtless *and* inappropriate—the latter behaviors I find more prevalent in friends who are cisgender, heterosexual males. It's a question of navigating physical and sexual boundaries. I suspect that this is because many men have what has been called a male sexual over-perception bias. This means that a man who is friends with a woman may misinterpret a friendly gesture or hug she gives him as being indicative of sexual interest, when it's not meant that way at all. So, in these relationships it's important to be clear about laying down firm ground rules, which I admit is often hard to do, because such gestures are often ambiguous. But, then again, sometimes they are not ambiguous at all.

Like that time my married Australian guy friend came to the United States for a project. I didn't have room for him in my apartment, so I arranged for him to stay with a mutual friend. One evening when the three of us had dinner together, while the hosting friend was in the kitchen and the Aussie friend was saying goodbye to me at the door, he made a truly inappropriate gesture—he patted and squeezed my bottom. I shoved him away and glared. I had my backpack purse over my shoulder, so I then wondered if perhaps his hand hadn't just slipped. But, no, there was that squeeze—and, besides, he'd done this when our other friend was out of the room. Now, of course, inspired by the #MeToo movement, I would have no problem saying, "I'm really disappointed in you for doing something so inappropriate. Don't do it again."

After he left town, we didn't stay in contact—because of distance more than anything—yet I can see that if we had stayed in touch, I would have needed to express how I felt about his inappropriate gesture. It's by bringing an issue like this to light that we can help shift entrenched behavioral patterns. And our friendships are a great forum in which to talk about what's appropriate and what isn't. This will vary greatly from person to person, which is one reason that it's so worthwhile to get a friend's perspective—as we explored in chapter 3 when we looked at biases. Basically, thoughtless and inappropriate behavior shows a lack of understanding. So, rather than assuming that you already know how a friend feels about what they've done, it's often important to ask them—and to listen to what they have to say.

And then, there are times when you need to curtail listening to a friend.

SHE SUCKED THE LIFE OUT OF ME

"I never, ever stopped loving her," my friend Amelia confessed, remembering a time when her fun-loving college friend and traveling buddy, Rosalie, was slowly disintegrating into a sea of booze and pain.

Amelia then spoke about how Rosalie "would get off work on a Friday night and start drinking in her garage. She'd sit there, drunk and call me depressed, crying, complaining. I'd hate picking up those calls. She sucked the life out of me, calling while drunk at all hours."

At the time, Rosalie probably felt she had a lot to complain about. She was caring for two toddlers and she resented her gloomy husband. "Her drinking *caused* her marital problems and got between many relationships." Amelia said. "The phone calls with Rosalie never changed and it was like the definition of insanity—doing the same thing over and over and expecting a different result." And while Amelia felt sad for her friend, she couldn't resolve Rosalie's problems, and certainly wasn't resolving them by listening to her nonstop complaining.

"You don't have enough time in your life," Amelia said. "I'm raising kids, I'm working full time, and I have a home to keep up. Everything beyond that has to be something I choose to do."

With thoughts like these, Amelia saw that she wanted the people in her life to be "uplifting, positive, and growing friends." She added, "People will need a shoulder to cry on every once in a while." On the other hand, "If they can't get out of this and do something for themselves, I don't have time for it. I don't have the energy." So, after hours of serving as Rosalie's emotional dumping ground and having her suggestions of therapy ignored, Amelia stopped engaging in Rosalie's marital drama by not returning her calls. A clear boundary.

And setting a friendship boundary in this way does not mean that this friendship is gone forever. Rosalie moved through her problems. She got sober and went back to college, receiving a master's degree in education. Years later, when her life was back on track, she tentatively reached out to Amelia, and the two of them connected once again—this time in a wonderful way.

However, it may not always turn out this way. Often our pessimistic friends keep that state of mind no matter what. According to Jason Moser, a psychology professor at Michigan State University, there's pretty good evidence that there's a biological component to negative thinking patterns.[1] So, it's possible that this tendency contributes to your friend's negative outlook.

And at times, you may feel like saying to this friend, *Come on, why don't you just snap out of it!* But Moser found in his research studies that negative thinkers can't *just snap out of it!* "Their minds, their brains, have a harder time generating positive thoughts," Moser explained. "They are not easily unstuck from this pattern."[2]

In other words, the negative thought patterns that might look like a character flaw are often a function of the physiological brain. It's not imagined; it's just the way their brain works.

We may want to show our support, love, and patience with friends who have pessimistic tendencies; however, if we're going to stay connected with them, it's important to be realistic. And that means setting boundaries. Think of these boundaries as social protocols to protect your own energy. Here are some ideas to practice:

- *Set a time limit.* Whether it's a coffee date or a phone call, let your friend know how much time you can give them right now, and stick to it. For a one-on-one conversation, using the phone or video conferencing to connect gives you more control over your time.
- *Include other people.* Invite several people to the same event. You can catch up with a group of people, and this way it's less likely you'll be corralled into a one-sided conversation.
- *Book an activity.* Go to a museum, a swap meet, a movie, a play, a book discussion—giving yourselves another focus for your get-togethers.

These are just some of the ways to offer support to a friend who tends to be pessimistic without leaving yourself feeling drained.

Even if a friend doesn't have a negative tendency, we may find there are many issues that arise when we believe a friend crosses a boundary.

MANAGING BOUNDARIES

Many times I've heard myself and others say things like this:

She should already know how I feel!
It's common knowledge that it happens that way!
How could he think that was anything but an insult!
She is always prying into my business!
He seems to expect so much of me!

Because we can't read each other's minds, it's worth turning our frustra-tions—our feelings of being off-balance, guilty, angry, or upset—into actions. These actions are about communicating the value we place on our own time and space, without being rude or unkind. I have five specific suggestions.

1. *Limit your social interactions with this person.*
   I had a friend who constantly talked about her life, a life I wasn't much interested in—such as how drunk she got, and the guys she picked up. This woman was not someone with whom I felt comfortable sharing private information. On the other hand, she was fun, an associate friend with many insightful ideas. So, we would set up a one-on-one coffee date, and when I arrived, I'd let her know I had another activity planned in an hour—giving myself what we call in television a "hard out."

2. *Clarify your position—even if it introduces social distance.*
   My friend Camila told me that when her daughter was an in-fant, her close friend Lizzie would still call Camila about going clubbing after 10:00 p.m.—like she had in the old days. On one occasion, when Lizzie was having birthday party, she was especially insistent. Camila said, "Talk to any of your friends with children. They'll tell you the same thing. I'm up at 2:00, 3:00, 5:00 a.m. with my baby. And I need to be here. You'll have plenty more birthdays when I will be able to come. And I'm still there for you in other ways." Even so, Lizzie stopped calling, and their friendship went into hibernation. Until, that is,

Lizzie moved in with her sister, who had young children running around. She then called Camila and apologized. "I didn't know," Lizzie said. And they picked up their relationship again.

3. *Name your boundaries—even small ones.*

A former roommate always had milk in the fridge, and sometimes, when I ran out of milk myself, I'd use hers. One day, I was having tea with a colleague at the kitchen table, when my roommate stormed in, grabbed the almost empty milk carton off the table, and waved it dramatically in my face, saying, "This is mine, all mine!" As it happened, this time it wasn't *hers, all hers.* Later, I told her that and also addressed her rude dramatics. I did, however, hear her complaint loud and clear—and I knew I was guilty as charged. I apologized, and to avoid bad feelings in the future, we set up a jar for milk money. The issue never came up again. This may seem like a tiny matter, but by managing these mini boundaries, you can gain excellent practice for handling the bigger, more challenging violations when these arise.

4. *Reset boundaries by resetting yourself.*

I have a few friends who are self-proclaimed people pleasers, and—no surprise—they have great difficulty setting clear boundaries. My friend Samuel, whom I mention in chapter 2, wanted validation from others and left himself open to being manipulated by them. As he put it, "I was a control freak; I wanted to control what people thought of me," but that validation came at a cost. It took him years of personal work—in therapy, with Co-Dependents Anonymous (CoDA)—to realize that he had an issue, and that he needed to manage himself better. He had to look after his own needs, before the needs of others. And he learned that by setting boundaries, a friendship may end—and he can't control that. To help with this process he wrote out what he'd say if someone asked for something he didn't want to do, then reread and practiced his role. If he were asked to do something, he'd embark on a process called HALT in which he would ask himself, "What am I feeling?" If it turned out that he was *hungry, angry, lonely,* or *tired,* then he would take that into account in deciding how to respond. He described HALT as a way of being honest with yourself and of learning "how to manage, not control, the people in your life."

5. *Be willing to end the friendship.*

This is a tough one, ending a friendship. The topic came up during my interview with an executive coach, Barry Collodi, and he said, "I called a friend just a few years ago who I thought had behaved badly and wasn't in communication after an act of generosity on my behalf. I said, 'Tina, I have to tell you I think we've played our friendship out. And I'm ending it now.' And, she said, 'I don't know what to say,' and I said, 'I knew you wouldn't, which is one of the reasons I'm ending this.' And I never heard from her again. There was no attempt to build the bridge, which means I got it right."

Be courageous in your friendships; I believe courage is contagious—in a good way! And bear in mind that there are times when a friend situation can really get out of control.

DANGEROUS LIAISONS

Occasionally, I've had friends who started behaving in ways that are not good for them—and consequently not good for me. In this sort of situation, even an essential friend can drift downward on the scale of closeness over time. Maybe they're getting drunk every night, doing hard drugs, or they've taken up with someone who is dangerous. You may feel guilty about abandoning your friend, especially if you believe they're facing a real threat. However, it's important to protect yourself from these scenarios, even though the situation can be complex. In fact, it almost always is complex.

For the drinking and drugs, I want to point out that Al-Anon and Nar-Anon offer support for the friends and family of alcoholics and drug addicts. If you have such a friend and you want to stay in contact with them, one way to protect yourself is to enter one of these support groups. This way you can get information about the behaviors that often come up for people with these issues—and learn some suggested strategies for handling these behaviors.

I know what it feels like when you suddenly feel threatened by a friend's behavior. Once, out of the blue, I got a call from a menacing bail bondsman who was looking for Craig—yes, the same guy who'd wanted me to work on spec from earlier in the chapter. Apparently, Craig owed this bondsman a lot of money, and the guy wanted it back. Today.

So I phoned Craig and asked why a bail bondsman was calling my number. Craig told me that one night he'd been drinking and found himself running late for a meeting. At his exit on the freeway, the ramp was blocked by a line of bright orange cones. Getting angry at this, Craig hit the gas and smashed through the cones—and straight on past a couple of cop cars. Yep, he got busted on a DUI and gave *my* contact information to the bail bond dealer.

"You're my rock," Craig told me.

I told him that I was willing to be his rock but that I wouldn't let him erode me. I told him to get back to that bondsman immediately, to give him the right contact information—Craig's own phone number—because I never wanted to receive a call like that again.

Once more: a boundary. And Craig did get it sorted out. That very day.

I have to admit that working in the artistic and creative world probably means setting more boundaries with friends than if I were in banking or real estate. Whatever arena you play in, however, it's up to you to be vigilant about not allowing anyone you hang out with to take you down a path you don't want to travel. You don't want a friend who's medicating their problems with alcohol or a conman in your life or a cranky bail bondsman calling you. Yet I feel it's also important that if this person does get back on track—whether this means getting sober or getting rid of some adverse association—you give your former friend the space to come back into your life.

· 10 ·

Honesty

Telling Difficult Truths

*W*hen I was a producer on the syndicated daytime talk series *The Montel Williams Show*, one of the most enjoyable parts of my job was interviewing prospective guests. I met an array of people who had a variety of perspectives on life, and a number of these conversations have stayed with me today. One was with the late therapist Paul Pearsall, who was adamant that we must always tell the truth. He told me, "Don't lie! Don't lie! Don't lie!" If I *did* lie, Pearsall said, I would divorce sooner and die younger. "Even your dog will die younger," he said. I'm not sure if he mentioned a cat.

When he appeared on *Montel*, Pearsall sat by himself on the stage, and audience members asked him questions that all seemed to begin with the words "Am I lying if—?" They filled in the blank with matters ranging from "I tell my friend she looks cool in a dreadful red dress?" to "I don't tell my partner I've cheated on him?"

Pearsall's answers to the above were yes and yes. Both, he said, would be a conscious intention to deceive another.

I had always thought of myself as a pretty straight shooter, but after taking in Pearsall's no-nonsense, no-holds-barred approach to honesty, I became more determined about telling the truth. Only when I began doing research on honesty for *Better You, Better Friends: A Whole New Approach to Friendship* did I realize there are a few caveats regarding across-the-board honesty—for instance, attempting to get out of a dangerous situation. Also, the importance of distinguishing facts from opinions, whether they're other people's or your own.

And I discovered that there is a big difference between the various forms of dishonesty. *Deception*, the umbrella term, covers omitting, editing, or avoiding a troubling truth, as well as falsehoods, bald-faced lies, or complete whoppers—which are all straight-up fiction. But deception comes in different guises. In this chapter, we'll look at several of these:

- Offering your personal opinions
- Being the messenger of other people's assessments
- Sharing information about a third person (that's difficult for the person hearing it)
- Sharing information about yourself (that you feel is compromising)

And we'll also look at how we, as human beings, are hardwired to believe what we're told. Let's start with how to navigate subjective truths—opinions.

OFFERING YOUR OPINIONS

Opinions are discussions about taste, ideas, or personal philosophy and don't necessarily rely on hard facts or objectivity. If you and a friend agree on an idea, taste, and so on, the two of you feel validated, connected, and have relationship harmony. If, however, your opinion differs from a friend's, you get to find out how the two of you deal with these differences. Doing this gracefully is more supportive of a friendship than agreeing on everything.

A friend raised four questions as a way to share her ideas on how to give honest, helpful opinions to others, and I found them to be both clear and relatable:

1. *Is your opinion in response to a question?* Has your friend actually solicited your opinion? If not, then often the best route is to keep quiet. There are times with very good friends (and I talk about one of these later) when it can be important to share your opinion, even if it hasn't been sought. Most of the time,

however, you're probably better off keeping your unsolicited opinion to yourself. I had an experience like this when I was in my twenties. One evening, I got a bit tipsy at a party and was pretty forward with an attractive man. The next day a friend told me that I'd made fool of myself. I felt terrible—until, that is, I found out she'd been interested in the same guy. *Hmmm.* I hadn't asked for her opinion, and what *was* her motivation in giving it?

2. *Does this person truly want my opinion?* I love the saying, *If I want your opinion, I'll give it to you!* Because if a friend is clearly pleased by his new shirt, then I don't have to chime in that, though I love the colors, the pattern is too busy for my taste. He may even have said, "What do you think of my new shirt!" but you *know* when this isn't a question, when he's really just saying, *This is a new shirt!* In this case, I'd say the part that works for me— "The color brings out your eyes"—even if the pattern turns me off. Be tactful, especially if he loves the look. Although I will say that if you have a *very close* friendship and the two of you have set up honesty rules, then you may pipe in with your opinion about the cluttered pattern.

3. *Would my opinion improve the situation?* One of my friends is on the internet dating scene, and she'll ask my opinion occasionally about this or that guy, especially one who's not returning her calls. I'll say something like, "Well, you know him, and I don't, so what do you think this means?" Then I try to guide her into forming her own conclusion about what's going on. I don't know the guy. Maybe's he's busy working or traveling, or maybe he's a lothario, but for me to automatically speculate about his behavior or the situation isn't helpful or informative. However, helping her find clarity around the situation herself is constructive.

4. *How can I deliver my opinion so that this person is likely to be able to take it in?* When you're sharing an opinion that might not be easy for someone to hear, sometimes you might be especially tactful—and sometimes I find it helps to be funny and light. I certainly appreciate humor myself. Like the time my fashionista

buddy was quite candid when giving me his opinion of the tight, tan dress I had tried on for a big TV event. He said, "You look like a sausage!" I laughed. How could I not laugh! And thank goodness he was there. Not only for his honest opinion, which of course I took to heart, but also so he could help me peel out of the thing.

What I love about these small exchanges of opinion with a friend is that they reveal a lot about our relationship. When receiving a friend's opinion, I look at how it's being offered. When I'm considering how to deliver my own opinion, I ask myself if my friend is open to hearing what I have to say. I try to discern when I should be honest and when I should zip it—when, for instance, my opinion is irrelevant or unhelpful or possibly even hurtful. And when I do share my perspective, afterward I ask myself if that tendered opinion turned out to be helpful.

These small communications are the foundation to the next level of trust—where higher stakes may be involved.

DON'T KILL THE MESSENGER

One reason it's so tough to share difficult information is that it can hurt the other person's feelings or even make them angry. Sometimes you don't have a choice about delivering a difficult message—an opinion—to a friend. The opinion may not be yours alone; you may have been drafted to pass it along. In this case, you're a messenger, which is tricky position to be in. There is a reason for the idiom *Don't kill the messenger*—because killing the bearer of bad tidings has been going on since ancient Greece! Let me tell you a story.

I first met my friend Marcus when we were both taking an evening playwriting course at a local university. We enjoyed working together and, preparing for a big play competition, he directed my play and I his. Marcus was hugely talented and working in a dead-end job. What he needed, he told me, was that one chance to get into the entertainment business. So, when I landed a job as a researcher for a comedy talk show and they needed a production assistant, I put his name forward. He was hired.

At first, he was thrilled and worked very hard. Then he seemed to get an attitude—he was a few years older than I, and he began to feel that being a production assistant (copying scripts, running errands, organizing supplies) was beneath him. The PA is, generally speaking, a *gofer* with a title. Marcus began to refuse to copy scripts and complained when he had to go on a production run. After a while, my boss—*our* boss— told me to talk to Marcus because if he didn't change his demeanor, he'd be fired. So, this was a really tough message—both for me to deliver and for him to receive.

On my end, I did the best I could to be both clear and positive. I told Marcus that his behavior on the job was hurting his performance, yet he was talented enough that, if he changed his attitude, he could be promoted. Marcus was furious with me. He said I was lording my position over him and sabotaging his career. The next day, he stopped talking to me.

Soon after, the show was canned, and Marcus and I lost contact— until about a year later, when I received a beautiful letter from him. He wrote that he now realized I was the one person who'd given him a chance. Marcus apologized for his behavior. He told me he was now living in another state, where he could start over, and that he'd always remember our friendship. There was no return address.

Marcus's thoughtful letter meant a lot to me. He was saying that our friendship had ended because of his misunderstandings and not my unpleasant message. Of course, our friendship *had* still ended—but it needn't have happened that way. And to illustrate this, let me tell you another story, one where I received the difficult message.

Once when I was looking for a TV project, my friend Tucker was working with a couple of TV executives who needed a segment producer. He promised to get me in if he could. A couple of days later Tucker called to say, "They don't want anyone from the Writers Guild; it's not in their budget." OK, it sucked, but what can you do!

Then, these execs hired a colleague with the exact same WGA credential as mine. At the time I found this odd but concluded that they'd probably changed their minds. A few weeks later, a mutual friend told me that Tucker had lied. And not only that, he had actively campaigned against my getting the job.

Quite honestly, if this other person hadn't told me what had really happened, I probably would have never suspected the truth. In this case, I reevaluated my friendship with Tucker, and saw that the deliverer of bad tidings had shown her loyalty to me—and that's why she and I remain essential friends to this day.

You might wonder why it was my initial response to trust what each of these people told me. It turns out we're hardwired for trust.

BELIEVING WHAT WE HEAR

When we receive information, we tend to believe it, at least for the short term. This is a finding of Timothy Levine, the University of Alabama (UA) communications professor we met in the last chapter. Levine's research has been funded by the National Science Foundation, the U.S. Department of Defense, and the FBI. As he explained to me, "The advantage goes to the liar."[1] This is because people, generally, are really bad at detecting lies in real time. Levine said, "We tend to discover lies after the fact." And, of course, if lies continue to accumulate, then you know you have a problem with this friend.

So why is it so hard to detect deceptions at the moment we're given them?

Levine has come up with what he calls *the truth default theory*, which is that our default setting as human beings is to believe what others tell us—"at least momentarily, at least usually."[2] Levine explained this by saying that we're a highly social species and that, for the sake of efficient communication and coordination, it's important for us to believe friends, family, coworkers, and so on. "Can you imagine having a friend that you had to second-guess everything they said? They couldn't be a friend, right? We couldn't have close, trusting relationships on that basis."

Besides, he continued, being suspicious of everyone takes enormous effort. It's exhausting. "So, we're not suspicious," Levine said.

"This is our default passive belief. And we are this way unless we have reason to *be* suspicious."

Following Levine's line of reasoning, I was programmed to accept as fact what my friend Tucker had told me. After I learned the truth, I remembered how years earlier I had held back on telling him about landing a terrific contract. I'd been sworn to secrecy—told to tell only one person who would help me move. I had the opportunity to tell Tucker, but I decided against it. I wasn't sure if he'd honor my request for confidentiality. For years I'd been watching Tucker be less than honest in his communications—for instance, he'd promise to call people back with no intention of ever doing so. And the woman who told me about Tucker? I had never seen this person lie. These bits of background are something Levine called "contextualized communication."

With a troubling communication, he said, "If you understand elements of the context, you can start putting the story together, and start to assess its plausibility."

After I found out that Tucker lied to me about the TV project, we drifted apart for a few years, until eventually we circled back into each other's lives. But now I'm much more cautious about what I share with him when we get together. I choose to see Tucker's As—his generosity, his humor, his connection to much of my own world. I view him as an associate friend, and we happily chat about our mutual interests, which are often a lot of fun to discuss.

WHAT WE FAIL TO SAY

There may be times when you tell yourself that you're not *really* deceiving a friend—because you're not flat-out lying. But, in fact, you may be deceiving yourself on this, because if you're not telling your friend the whole *uncomfortable* truth, this too is a form of deception.

Levine defined a lie as a fabrication, a fiction, and in his research he found that to truly make something up in this way is quite rare. The most common deception is leaving out or obfuscating relevant information, what Levine called *avoidance lies*. These, he said, "are particularly common among friends."

One of Levine's colleagues at the University of Alabama, a professor who teaches classes on deceptive messages and communication in close relationships, told me that it's easy to manipulate our speech, leaving out those niggling little truths that our friends may feel are important to know. "That's the most the common form of deception," Steven McCornack said, "is just editing out problematic information."[3]

McCornack gave this example: just say your best friend goes to a party and hangs out with someone you can't stand. In fact, this person bad-mouthed you to your buddy. When you ask your buddy about the party, he decides to leave the part out the bad bits, right? Then, somehow you find out, and that's when, as McCornack said, "You're going to see your friend as having acted dishonestly," and you'd probably wonder why he didn't tell you.

Most of us say we want the unedited version of what happened, right? But sometimes when we hear the whole truth, it can be uncomfortable and embarrassing—and that's why we blame the messenger.

When I brought up these ideas with my longtime friend Nicole over eggs and toast at my favorite diner, she told me she knew I always wanted the truth and reminded me of something that had happened between us. It's similar to a story I told in chapter 5—yes, it happened again.

Years ago, on Saturday nights a group of us would meet at Bootius Maximus, which was, according to its flyers, an "African Caribbean RNB Hi, Hop Funk Dance Club Thang" in West Los Angeles. One evening, Nicole ended up at the club without me and ran into my then boyfriend, Sadler, who asked her out on a coffee date. Making it perfectly clear he wanted it to be just the two of them.

Nicole turned him down. More than this, she came to see me the next day, and told me what had happened. She took this risk to tell me because she felt that I would want to know—and that I wouldn't blame her, the messenger. She was right on both counts.

Now I'm going to apply the Nicole/Sadler scenario to the model McCornack outlines in his research study.[4] Here are three choices Nicole had when talking with me about what happened during that fateful night at the club. She could have told me . . .

- *A bald-faced lie:* She didn't make it to the club and instead decided to go to a movie with a coworker.
- *An edited version of the truth:* She saw Sadler, they had a dance, and then she didn't see him again—editing out his invitation.
- *The truth:* The whole thing, including the difficult part about Sadler asking her out on a date.

Nicole knew me well enough to feel she needed to deliver the unfiltered truth, and that's why she continues to be an essential friend today.

On the other hand, when I asked Sadler about this, he groaned and said Nicole had blown the whole thing out of proportion. He'd only wanted to find out more about *me* through her. Which, my friends, was a complete whopper, and one of the reasons we eventually parted ways.

THE HONESTY RULES

In a relationship class McCornack has been teaching for the last twenty-five years with his spouse, Kelly Morrison—also a professor of communication studies at UA—they stress that to have a successful relationship, it is fundamental to define honesty rules.

"And what *define honesty rules* means," McCornack added, "is that, regardless of the relationship whether it's a close friendship or romance, you need to have some kind of an agreement between the two of you regarding what you tell and what you don't tell."

For me, this point is highly significant. I have a pretty strong code of honesty with my friends, but as McCornack pointed out to me, "Your friend is not you!" That's when I realized I must not assume that my friends have the same code of honesty with me. So, the degree of honesty we want to observe with each other is something that, as friends, we need to talk over. What I especially like about this approach is that a discussion like this can open a whole new avenue of communication between you and your friends. I've had friends who want to know everything and others who appreciate privacy. One example comes to mind.

A few years back a friend went on an extended trip, and she knew that while she was away her fiancé had an affair. When he met her at the airplane, she told him, "I know you had an affair, and that's that. I'm back, and I never want to hear about it again." After this woman's friends heard what she said to her fiancé, we understood that bringing up this subject would be neither helpful nor kind. She had dealt with it privately. And within a year they were married.

Setting honesty rules is about being clear about what you want from someone. Then if a friend overshares, let them know. If a friend doesn't share enough, let them know that too.

McCornack said that both he and Morrison feel that honesty in a relationship—even in a close relationship and especially in a sexual relationship—does not necessarily mean telling your partner everything. To be honest is to be true to the agreement the two of you have negotiated between yourselves regarding what should be disclosed. "And you've *got* to negotiate that," McCornack added, "because if you don't, there are going to be violations and arguments about the violations—*You should have told me* or *You shouldn't have told me.*"

Telling the truth is about not deceiving another person. However, if you decide you don't wish to disclose something private about yourself to a friend, then don't. At the same time, if there's a lot of stuff you want to hide from a particular friend, then maybe that's a red flag in this relationship, especially if you consider this person an essential friend. You might ask yourself whether this friendship is still working for you.

HOW OPEN ARE YOU?

As our friends are voluntary, Levine noted, we probably have less need to deceive friends than we have to deceive our families. "It's the involuntary relationships that are more deception prone," he said. Friendship "provides a bit of immunization against deception. If you have lots and lots of reasons to deceive this person," he added, "maybe you just don't need to have them as a friend."

With coworkers, you're kind of stuck with them, and your family isn't going anywhere. "If I disagree with my parents," Levine continued, "I'm going to hide that. Because it's not going to turn out well." Yet if there's a problem in a voluntary relationship, it's easier to drop your connection with that person.

Which reminds me of the time decades ago when my friend Andre told the heterosexual couple he was living with at the time that he was gay. Unfortunately, he picked the wrong people to come out to. They were so shocked that they told Andre to pack his stuff and go! Immediately. He couldn't turn to his family of birth—they didn't know he was gay—so, he came to stay with my group of friends. I don't see myself as a heroic character in Andre's story, but my friends and I did help him out at a time when he needed that.

I love the statement made in an interview by the actor who played the Hot Priest in Phoebe Waller-Bridge's comedy series *Fleabag*: "Mercifully, these days people don't see being gay as a character flaw. But nor is it a virtue, like kindness. Or a talent, like playing the banjo. It's just a fact. Of course, it's part of my makeup, but I don't want to trade on it."[5]

On the other hand, if we feel we have to hide fundamental truths about our life from certain friends, then are these friendships worth having? I understand that there may be practical reasons for being cautious around colleagues. One of my media contacts told me that, when she is at work, she chats with her conservative coworkers about her "spouse," never mentioning that her spouse is a woman. But, as we've said, colleagues aren't people we necessarily choose, and while it's important to have a degree of affability at work, you don't have to be intimate with people on the job. You may become friends with them, but you don't have to; you just have to work with them. Social friends are another matter.

I share a lot with my essential friends. They give me honest and loving feedback—and vice versa. They know I keep their secrets, and I know how loyal they are to me. With collaborators, I share less. With associate friends I focus on our common interests, and I'm a lot less likely to share my private information.

As a culture, we overshare—but be clear that's often more about being noticed than it is about being honest. I almost had to put a gag order on one friend who would reveal way too much about her health issues and past sex life when she was on a first date. Yikes! I shy away from people who overshare, those who mindlessly blurt out far too much information. Or tell another's secrets. It's as if, for these people, information is social currency, something that gives them power in a group, rather than a means of seeking enduring companionship.

Before sharing your all, let the friendship unfold naturally through trust. See if it's a good match. Let each friendship breathe and find its own rhythm.

So, when I remember Pearsall's saying let's find ways to be more honest with each other, it opens up a whole new field of experience with friends: nurturing trust through our differences, being a courageous and loving messenger, and finding friends with whom you can be candid. Set honesty boundaries that work for you, even if they differ from a friend's.

In this chapter, we've examined some differences between our work and social friends. Many of us, however, have met our closest friends at the office. This is certainly true for me. And it makes sense: we have a common interest with these folks—our career—and a lot of access to get to know them.

Yet developing friendships in a work environment can be tricky. So, next we'll look at how to navigate these precarious, and possibly rewarding, relationships.

Friends at Work

$\mathscr{P}$hil was an entertaining, irreverent work pal, always amusing me with behind-the-scenes shenanigans from other shows he'd been with. We worked together on a pilot and after that I asked him to coproduce a couple of pitches with me. Even when we weren't on the same project, Phil would help me out. He'd email me a television budget template. He'd give me candid feedback about a production contract or talent deal. Occasionally, he'd create a funny limerick about me at work. It was always fun to open an email from him and read, "There once was a lady from Down Under." They were hilarious.

Yet with all of this, Phil always declined my networking and social invitations to him and his wife. And, quite honestly, it baffled me. We were friends, weren't we?

So, one day I called my pal Anton to ask him what he thought, and Anton walked me through a set of questions that clarified my situation with Phil. Since I work in television, I thought it would be appropriate to script the conversation I had with Anton on this topic:

ANTON

What is it you want Phil to do?

GLENDA

Well, help with the business side. Do the budgets, get traction with clients.

ANTON

And is he doing that?

GLENDA

Yes, but he never offers networking opportunities or introduces me to his wife.

ANTON

Why would he introduce you to his wife?

GLENDA

Because we've known each other for years! We're friends!

ANTON

What's that got to do with knowing his wife? Who do you call if you need a budget template?

GLENDA

Phil.

ANTON

Is he cool about it when you ask for business stuff like that?

GLENDA

(sheepishly)

Yes.

ANTON

Sometimes you have to pigeonhole people. You've got a great thing going with Phil. Don't wreck it by expecting him to invite you to come home with him! This guy serves you well. Concentrate on that.

GLENDA

Is this your idea of a friend?

ANTON

A friend? I don't know—but it's good policy. And you won't drive yourself crazy expecting more from someone than he's willing to offer!

So, Anton's point was that my cohort Phil had set down clear boundaries between his work and home life. It took Anton's pointing this out for me to get it. I've thought about this a lot over the years. I haven't worked with Phil for quite a while, but I'm pretty sure he'd help me out in business if he could. That was significant for me to take in. Regardless of what this colleague *doesn't* want to offer, he adds enormous value to my life. It's up to me to manage my expectations of him by appreciating all that this relationship provides me.

This raises an interesting question: what is an appropriate professional friendship? Barry Collodi, who's an executive coach for Fortune 500 companies, suggested that the answer is different for every person. As Collodi said when I interviewed him, we all ask ourselves questions like these: "How much of myself do I want to put out there? How much social time do I want to invest?" He added, "If I'm married, and I've got four kids, and I live an hour's commute away, I'm not going drinking with the gang more than, maybe, once a month."[1] For someone in this situation, work friends are colleagues and home is a different matter entirely.

So, it's important to be clear about your own circumstances, to honor the circumstances of your colleagues.

For years, it was quite different for me. After leaving home and moving to Adelaide to go to university, and then living overseas, I rarely had my family around. And working in the entertainment industry, with its long hours and erratic schedules, I often felt the people I worked with were my family (warts and all)—at least for the time of the project. We'd develop a verbal shorthand and insider jokes as we grappled with changing itineraries and frustrating budgets. Occasionally, I'd meet someone with whom I really clicked, and we became lifelong, essential friends.

After I married, I needed to balance my home life with my work obligations. Even though I didn't have children, I now had a home life, which was more grounded than my previous social life had been.

For people raising children or dealing with the illness of one at home, there can be a significant need to separate work and home. The demands of home may be even greater than the demands of work.

And even if it's not like that for a person, everyone has their own idea of what it means to maintain parity between work and home. As I mentioned in chapter 4, one of my breakthrough moments was seeing that I envied a colleague because she had a balanced life between her career and family—which, at the time, I didn't have.

GENDER QUESTIONS

The idea of mixed genders working together in an office is a new construct in our history—especially as peers. So, it's not surprising that each gender brings different, innate behaviors toward friendship into the company. Scholars have written research papers exploring how women enjoy what would be considered more familial, intimate friendships, whereas men's friends tend to be more functional. Males put a higher premium on friends "who are athletic, have good financial prospects, and are socially well connected." These attributes differ from females who value "traits indicative of intimacy potential, such as kindness, compassion, and empathy."[2]

Our ancestral mothers engaged in "cooperative breeding"—creating a mutually beneficial environment to provide the best resources for their children; forming close, "kin and non-kin" bonds.[3] So it interested me when Collodi discussed one of his clients, Marina Maher Communications, which, he told me, "is about 90 percent women over two hundred people. And they've built the most remarkable culture, which accommodates and has flexibility to individual needs—at every level in the organization. So, if I'm an account executive who just had a child, I'm probably going to work from home or even take one day off during the week. And there are very few hidden agendas, like you find in most companies. It's very collaborative, very cooperative. High levels of respect and respectful communication."

Men, on the other hand, band together to protect their tribe against attacking interlopers, and this "out-group defence called for coalitional cooperation and behaviour"[4]—which interested me as recently I had dinner with a male friend who recalled once working in an all-male environment. He had a buddy who was a truly kindhearted sort—just, well, a little quirky. So all the guys in the office banded together to protect him so he'd keep his job. But, that band of brothers all moved on, leaving the guy exposed to a new manager, who eventually let him go. My friend was outraged. *Why didn't they help him? He's such a great person!* When I asked if he'd talked to his quirky pal recently, my friend gazed at me seemingly a little confused for a moment, then said, "I don't have his number and wouldn't know how to reach him." Even though they were close buds, they didn't stay connected.

These expressions of friendship also align with the categories I discussed earlier in the book. Women tend toward collaborator friends, seeking emotional connections that provide support at work. And men are more likely to seek associates, forming bonds through a common goal or project. As a frequently quoted research study states, "Common usage now characterizes women's same-gender friendships as 'expressive,' 'communal,' or 'face-to-face' and men's same-gender friendship as 'instrumental,' 'agentic,' or 'side-by-side.'"[5] In the prevailing research prior to the early 1990s, women were found to be predominantly "expressive," rather than "instrumental." Yet, in this research paper the authors concluded that, while nothing changed in the men's behavior toward each other, they found "that women's friendships tend to be both expressive and instrumental."[6]

I have to wonder if women are adapting to multi-gender workplace situations, now they're often employed outside the family. When my sister was working—she's retired now—she had a similar approach to my colleague Phil and possibly her male ancestors. Elaine made it quite clear that her work friends were colleagues while her social friends and her family were home base. She was unapologetic about those boundaries. "I'd go to lunch with the people I worked with," she told me, "but I'd really have to consider invitations to dinner or other events with them, if they weren't work related."

One of the reasons Elaine had for making these clear distinctions is that she was an executive, and she wanted to avoid showing favoritism.

AN UNLEVEL PLAYING FIELD

The concern about favoritism is one of the strongest reasons against making friends with your boss or, if you're a boss, with one of your employees. Either way, this has its own unique set of issues. If your friendship is evident to others in the office, it may feel demoralizing to them. With such a friendship, there can easily be a perception of favoritism—and, with what we learned in chapter 3 about biases, I have to say that even when we think we're being fair, we may not be.

Besides, what happens when this boss/employee friendship sours? Now, you may suddenly feel vulnerable. You may *be* vulnerable. We hear about this with romantic relationships in the office but rarely about when a friendship goes belly-up.

It could happen that a boss might "befriend" you, making you feel pressure to socialize with them even though you would prefer not to. In that case, you would need to set your boundaries without naming them as such. You can say something like this: *Thank you for your lovely invitation this weekend, but I've already made plans.* Or if your super friendly boss is asking you to pick up more projects or increase your role far beyond what you were hired to do, you would need to use diplomacy. Offer a solution, something such as *I'm excited to create X, but I won't have time to do that and finish Y. So who would you want me to pass Y on to?*[7]

It can also happen that one of your colleagues is promoted from your peer group to manager. Are you suddenly going drop that person as a friend? I hope not. However, Collodi said, "I think it's very important that early on, before there are any issues, for the two parties to sit down and talk expectations and boundaries." What is the implication of your being friends in light of this new work role? What do the two of you have to address or take care of in order for this to be smooth?

Collodi suggested having this discussion ahead of time, because your friendship is important to you and so is your career. If you're the one who's the new manager, you don't want to show favoritism; you want the other members of the team to feel as if they're being treated fairly and have an opportunity to grow. But as Collodi noted, anything you do to "level the playing field" might be misunderstood by your friend. "You may need to be able to discuss those times, and also put some guidelines in."

FRIENDS-IN-OFFICE PROTOCOLS

We spend lots of time with people at work, and it's inevitable we'll make friends. There is, however, a difference between making friends socially and making friends at work. Here's a list of things to watch out for—insights from Barry Collodi and my sister Elaine as well as from me. Problems can come up when you do any of the following:

- *Oversharing:* Be careful to not share too much of yourself too soon, and be wary of someone who overshares with you too quickly. Let a friendship unfold.
- *Wasting time:* If your friend likes to chat in the office, they're probably wasting your time and disrupting your workflow. Meet them in the kitchen at your break for coffee; define *your* time.
- *Gossiping:* Don't do it, ever. If a colleague spreads gossip, let them know you're not interested, in a polite way. (You don't want to become their target.) Remember, demeaning, personal gossip against another is an act of aggression and a form of harassment.
- *Taking advantage of:* Don't expect a friend to either cover for you or do extra stuff—making them the designated lunch driver or expecting them to stay late to cover your weekly hair appointments. And if they impose on you, just say, "No, that's not possible today." That will get them out of the habit of asking without feeling criticized by you or frustrated with you—either of which could cause a personal or professional rift.
- *Being too personal:* Cheek-kissing and hugging a friend at work, as well as laughing together at insider jokes or sharing personal information, may alienate others in the office. So it's a good policy to leave your private friend affections outside your business lives.

SETTING DOWN GUIDELINES

I wish I'd put some guidelines in place with my friend Fred before I hired him to do research for me. In retrospect, I see that I needed to set up the same sort of professional agreement and safeguards that I would have put in place for a stranger. We looked at various ways to formalize money agreements between friends in chapter 6. Think about it. Work and money are not that different; work usually involves money. And for this particular friend and myself, when our business deal went sour, we almost lost our friendship.

Fred and I had first become friends on a sweltering Sunday afternoon, when we were both working overtime for a weekly publication. I was the arts and entertainment editor, and Fred wrote ad copy—although he wanted to write music reviews. So, on that particular day, when Fred rushed in to tell me that a famous rock keyboardist had just phoned and was willing to give the paper an interview, I told him to go do it.

Fred found out that this dude was a dud; he was impersonating the famous musician. "He doesn't even look like him," Fred said, frowning. "He has short hair, and holes in his socks. Nicky Hopkins wouldn't do that. Or maybe he would—but not in a Motel 6. Nicky would flop out at a Waldorf or a Standard." After that, Fred and I became fast friends.

Later, he told me: "You reached out to me. I was intimidated. I was next to the writers, and all the sudden. . . . I was in an environment I didn't think I belonged in, but you made me feel welcome." And, he said, because he felt welcomed and included by me, he could establish friendships with the others on the staff as well.

A few years later, through various twists and turns, a colleague hired me onto the start-up production for *The Montel Williams Show*, and a year after that, the show moved to New York—and I was invited to go too. At the time, I was writing a screenplay in my spare time about an eighties girl band ditching their suburban lives to reunite on a Route 66 comeback tour. I didn't have time to drive along Route 66 to do the necessary research, so I called Fred to find out if it was something he'd like to do for money. He'd always loved girl groups, especially the ones from the eighties.

I knew that Fred had drinking issues, and I asked him how he was doing. He assured me he was nine months sober, and that's when we agreed on a price—$1,500.00. Then, as soon as he got the money, Fred took a third of it to pay off his outstanding bills. This didn't sit well with me, and I told him so. That was the bankroll for this project and not fodder for the people he owed money to. Fred pointed out that he had to pay his bills to get out of town. Even though this was a huge red flag for me, I didn't listen to myself and call off the project, because Fred assured me that the rest of the money would last the distance—and I believed him.

Once he hit Route 66, Fred called me each night, regaling me with hilarious stories of various characters. He played bingo with local Apaches and Daughters of the American Revolution in a small-town hall; he met people who ran curio shops; he laughed with a grizzled bar owner. "I ordered Shirley Temples," he quickly assured me. But before he was more than one state into the interior of the continent—in Arizona to be precise—his calls stopped.

Days rolled by, and there was no phone call from Fred. On one hand, I really had to wonder what he was up to; on the other hand, I started to worry—a lot. Eventually the worry outweighed my skepticism, and I decided to telephone Fred's mom and then the sheriff in Fred's last port of call.

The next day Fred called, desperately sorry about not contacting me sooner. He explained that he'd been ashamed of himself. "All the money is gone," he said. His car broke down, and he got lost near Laughlin, Nevada—which is not even on Route 66. So, he went into town "to make some money to finish the trip." He had gambled away all the rest of my money in Laughlin, and had, right now, only $10.00 in his pocket. It was not enough to get him back to LA, and not enough money for him to stay in Laughlin.

After listening to his *I-really-screwed-up* soliloquy, I took a moment to breathe. Then I said, "I am really sorry that happened. But I expect you to pay me back all the money in full. And from now on, I'm charging you interest." Oh, and he'd have to find his own way back to LA.

I was furious with him—for blowing the opportunity *and* for blowing the money. Later, when we discussed what had happened, he told me "I approached the business arrangement like a friendship. When I lost the money, I was more disappointed in the friendship aspects of it rather than the business aspects. Because I let you down." Even so, it took him six years to pay back the money with interest. His last payment was delivered when he was performing in a movie in Los Angeles. He stayed with me during the production and also generously shared his paycheck treating friends to dinner. So, throughout all those years we did not lose our friendship. But until he paid it back, the money was, at times, an elephant in the room.

That business deal could have ruined our long-term friendship. Knowing what I know now about boundaries—and about Fred—I understand that, from the get-go, I needed to set down clear guidelines. What would those have been? Something like this:

- Say that the money was to be used directly for research.
- Pay him weekly, after he'd sent the last week's transcripts and pictures.
- Require him to give me the names of the people he met, their addresses, and their phone numbers.

With an agreement of that sort, Fred would have been kept accountable at each step of the project. He would have been clear that he was on Route 66 to do a job. There's a ubiquitous saying about the power of setting boundaries: *You teach people how to treat you.*

ADVANTAGES OF WORKING WITH FRIENDS

With all of these challenges I've been enumerating, I have to say that I still see a huge advantage of having a close friend—whether expressive or instrumental—in the workplace. Because, let's face it, most of us work long hours and we put significant energy into our jobs. Having a few close buddies at work can help you feel more productive and engaged. Work friends provide support and caring, and they give you perspective and feedback for the job you're doing—a great plus for me! Basically, they've got your back.

I know firsthand just how important it can be to have a friend at work. I was once in a very difficult work situation where, even before I turned on my computer for the first time, one of the other producers began gunning for my job. I saw what was happening and so did Ava, the friend who had hired me—how this other producer was gossiping about me, spreading half-truths, buttering up the show's Big Talent at my expense. I couldn't stop the other producer's destructive campaign, and there was nothing Ava could do to keep the inevitable from happening. After I'd been there five months, I lost my job.

Because I was working with a friend, however, I wasn't blindsided by being told at the last minute that I was fired. Ava had gotten her boss's permission to tell me early. And Ava told me in the most gracious way possible—at a lovely and very expensive. dinner set up by herself. Having a friend doesn't mean that you won't get fired. Your friend may still have to fire you, but if she's a friend—as Ava was—she'll do it with heart. And that's why Ava continues to be one of my essential friends today.

"What most people haven't figured out in a career path and in terms of friendship is just be the best of yourself," Collodi said. "If you just be yourself, not only will you build quality friendships, but you'll build them with the best people."

And to build quality friendships with the best people, we have to be able to *find* the best in ourselves so we can strengthen these bonds. A great friend, remember, starts with you—and that's what we discuss in the next chapter.

· 12 ·

Strengthening the Bonds of Friendship

*M*any of us have an idealized view of what friendship should look like. It's as if we're not living up to the picture we see in movies and ads and posted on social media—sometimes even on our own social media pages—and this can leave us feeling disconcerted or even embarrassed. I'd like to suggest another way of doing this: accept what's there.

This is something I learned from a revered art teacher, Bill Roode. Through our five years sketching and painting together, Bill continually said, "Really look at what you're seeing. Paint *that*. If her hand looks bigger than her head, paint it that way. It will give the painting perspective." He showed his students how there's more beauty and inspiration in painting the landscape or model's form with all the foreshortening and distortions, crags and folds, dark shadows and blotches than there is in painting a pretty picture that is your preconceived idea of what this should look like. "It's what you see that counts," he always said. "Not what you think it should look like."

I find this an inspiring metaphor for friendships, because if you're close to someone, it's very likely that it'll get messy at times, that problems will arise, and unexpected behaviors will come into play from both sides. Suddenly, your friend has found a new romantic partner, and you feel left out. Or he moved away and no longer calls—you're the one who generates all contact. Maybe you feel bad after seeing a close friend's social media shares of a party she gave that you knew nothing about.

COMMON COMPLAINTS ABOUT FRIENDS

Here are some common complaints about friends that you might spend some time rethinking.

1. *I do all the heavy lifting:* Often we claim that we're doing more of the "work" in a friendship, but is that a fact or is it our bias? Matthew Kugler, who spoke with me about bias in chapter 3, put it this way: "Part of the bias is making yourself look good, and another part of the bias is simply not being aware"—of how much your friend is really doing. And, yeah, sometimes a friend is busy with work or home, and you *may* have to do more to keep the connection alive. Make that a choice and less of a complaint.

2. *We're growing apart:* If this is something you're worried about, take action. But remember that sometimes "growing apart" is a natural part of life. She's leaving town for a job opportunity or spending much more time traveling; he's getting married or divorced. Being friends at age sixteen doesn't always work at thirty-six or sixty-six.

3. *I was excluded:* There are times you won't be invited to an event, so before you get huffy about why you weren't invited, get more information. Often it's unintentional— like the time my dear friend found out about my wedding through a change in my Facebook status, and immediately called me asking why I hadn't told her before I told the public! It was an oversight on my part. And if you discover it was intentional, then gauge the situation in a measured way—was it a small party? Have I reached out to her recently? Or are we growing apart?

4. *I've been dropped for a lover:* We all do this to our friends, even if we think we don't. Yet usually after the lust-and-dating period calms down, a few things can happen. The romance ends and your friendship goes back to the way it

was. Or the relationship lasts. If the relationship continues, you have a few choices. These include befriending the new partner or, if that isn't an option, reevaluating your expectations around the more limited time your close friend can now offer you. The range of choices can reflect your flexibility—your ability to shift into the next chapter of your relationship with a close friend.

5. *I like her more than she likes me:* Yes, this happens a lot. You consider someone an essential friend, and they consider you an associate. I think this may happen more if there's a perceived power differential—if, say, one person is more popular, more successful. So, as you can't change this other person's perception of you, manage your own expectations by enjoying what he or she has to offer you at this time. And if that isn't enough, find someone with whom you can have a more equitable friendship.

NOTE

This list was adapted from senior relationships reporter Brittany Wong's "Therapists Share the Friendship Issues People Complain About Most," *HuffPost*, July 7, 2018, https://www.huffingtonpost.com/entry/therapists-share-friendship-complaints_us_5b688dece4b0de86f4a3f5d4.

As I was writing this book, Bill Roode died, and this left me with some regrets. Bill and I had been friends when I was taking classes from him, but after he retired from teaching, we lost the thread of our friendship. When Bill had a stroke, his partner called to tell me. Now this man, who had always been so chatty and fun to hang out with, could barely speak. His partner and I set up a few dates for all of us to get together, but Bill was always too sick, and I got busy, so I didn't make much of an effort to stay connected. I meant to, but "meant to" doesn't cut it if you want to strengthen the bonds of friendship. Bill was dear to me, and now that he's gone, I'm sorry I won't have an opportunity to ever share that with him.

To avoid friendship regrets of this sort, it's worth investing some energy into deepening your bonds with friends. I've identified four areas that I think of as vital to becoming a more loving and realistic friend:

1. Address problems.
2. Listen and ask.
3. Take action.
4. Empathize on all levels.

Becoming more aware of the foreshortening and distortions, the crags and folds, the dark shadows and blotches in my friendships has helped me learn a lot about myself—some being lessons I hadn't realized I needed to learn.

ADDRESS PROBLEMS

In the past I was pretty open about what I shared with my friends. I was almost blasé about it. I didn't realize that sometimes a lot of information is too much information. Like the time years ago when I went away for a long weekend to a cabin in the mountains with my friend Shauna and her boyfriend, Rick. They had been living with each other for a few years, and even though I'd met Rick through Shauna, I was friends with both. Rick and I were buddies, with no sexual attraction. He was a stud—black-haired and green-eyed; he came from a wealthy family. Shauna adored Rick; I thought he was hilarious and inclusive—and we all got on. At some point Shauna had confided in me that Rick wasn't quite the lover her ex-beau had been.

So, here we were on our first day of the weekend. Rick and I decided to go canoeing, and Shauna didn't want to go. On our way to pick up the rental boats, Rick started bragging about how Shauna thought he was her best lover. And I raised my eyebrow, and said, "Really. That's not what she told me." I was teasing him about his braggadocio, though it's quite possible that I wanted to stick a pin into that inflated ego of his.

But now that I think about it, I have to ask myself, *how on earth could I say that!* Yet I did. Rick and I had a little banter about Shauna's ex, and then I forgot about all it. Rick, of course, did not.

When we got back to the cabin, he marched straight over to Shauna and said, "I'm the best lover you ever had, right? Glenda said something about your ex being better."

As soon as I saw Shauna's face, I realized I had breached a friend code. Her eyes flashed in shock; her face became red. She was furious with both of us, "What on—you discussed my sex life behind my back? I can't believe you did that! You have no right!"

I don't think I've seen her this mad, before or since. She was right. I had no right. I apologized profusely. And sincerely.

I had broken her trust. Rick may have been my friend, but he wasn't like just some other guy. He was Shauna's partner. She hardly spoke to me for the rest of that trip, and after we got back to the city, she cooled her heels for a while. Fortunately, she was vocal about how I'd broken her trust, and I heard her. She had addressed the problem clearly, and I persisted in reaching out to her, until eventually we got back together again. I'd have to say Shauna's an associate friend. We share a lot of history and, although we don't call each other much, if we happen to be in the same city, we'll get together for a friendly dinner date and talk about the old days. Rick is no longer in the picture.

I think it's important to pay attention to these kind of encounters with friends, rather than letting them slide by, because—friend alert!—just because you're close to this person, it doesn't mean they think like you or behave like you or communicate like you. One friend told me recently that throughout her entire adult life, she's had to deal with how she gives communications. "When I was young," she said, "I thought everyone was just like me. Then I began to see that people experience communication so differently." This woman is a straight shooter, and now she understands that "for some people a direct statement is like a body blow."

I agree. We all communicate differently. Including me, with my big mouth learning my "couple" lesson of a lifetime—don't get involved in a couple's private narrative, unless you're invited in or you observe really troubling, potentially dangerous behavior. In any event, think before you speak. I have endeavored to ever since. This incident was greatly beneficial for me. It helped me understand just how important it is in all our relationships to listen, think, and *then* respond when we're conversing with each other.

Listening may sound simple, but it's not.

LISTEN AND ASK

Just as important as seeing people—the lesson I learned in art classes so many years ago—is listening to them. Really listening to them. As an exercise in strengthening bonds of friendship, I like to practice what is known as active listening. This is listening with my full attention, without interrupting, so I can get an accurate read on what the other person is saying—and not thinking about a witty retort, or formulating my opinion/advice, or thinking *I wish they'd hurry up because I've got to go pick up my groceries.*

And let's be honest, you're not really strengthening your affinity with friends if you don't let them finish expressing their thought or sentence. Sometimes I barely start a sentence when the other person jumps in finishing my thought, expresses an opinion, or makes inaccurate assumptions. So, I've dramatized a conversation that could, for example, go something like this:

GLENDA

Oh, I've been meaning to tell you about—

FRIEND

That new restaurant, I heard it's not great.

GLENDA

No, no, my trip to Australia. We're planning on being there—

FRIEND

For the summer, right? That'll be nice.

GLENDA

No, for my sister's birthday. Her sons—

FRIEND

She's got a daughter about my daughter's age, right?

GLENDA

Nope. My nephews are throwing her a surprise party.

And I'm a pretty fast talker! Even so, a friend interjects her thoughts, ideas, and even a bit of her own biographical information. To be fair, I've done this many times myself. So the first step is to listen to each other's answers and points of view, without interruption.

If there's one sentiment you'd think would be innate to our behavior with friends, it's showing our interest through listening and asking questions. But, apparently, we don't seem to be able to find the time to fully engage with listening—and then we don't have enough information to ask questions. As I said, I've observed this personally and, in a 2017 Harvard research paper, a group of researchers came to the same conclusion—most of us are not good at asking questions, especially follow-up questions.

In a National Public Radio interview, NPR's social science correspondent Shankar Vedantam talks to one of the study's authors, Karen Huang, who explains, "I would meet someone for the first time, and I would actually be asking a lot of questions. And I noticed that the other person really enjoy[ed] talking about themselves and responding to my questions, but I would notice that they wouldn't really ask questions back."[1]

This was the heart of their findings, which were based on three studies.[2] Studies 1 and 2 tracked about six hundred online "getting-to-know-you" conversations, which, they say, clearly demonstrates that "people like their partners more when they ask more questions, because people who ask more questions are seen as more responsive."[3] And even though these conversations were with potential dates, I think they are relevant for friends as well.

Study 3, which I found particularly interesting, tracked more than one hundred speed daters who were gathered in three different round-robin introductory sessions. During these sessions each dater went on between fifteen and nineteen four-minute "dates," giving the researchers an opportunity to listen in on more than fifteen hundred conversations and gauge each from the two perspectives.

After the dates, everyone reported whether they wanted to go on a second date with the person they had just spoken with. Huang reports that the strongest indicator of whether someone was willing to go on a second date was the number of follow-up questions the other person had asked them.

Follow-up questions indicate you're listening to the other person, and that demonstrates responsiveness, which is a very likable trait. And, to no one's surprise, the fewer questions you ask, the less you're liked.

Alison Wood Brooks, an associate professor of business at Harvard and another researcher on this study, was fascinated by the issue of why people don't ask more questions.

What holds us back? In an article about this study,[4] Brooks offers her opinions, which include egotism—we're only focused on sharing our own ideas—or we don't want to appear rude, intrusive, or incompetent by asking questions. And the "darker reason," she suggests, may be that we just don't care what this person has to say.

To counter this, Brooks offers some solutions: "Think to yourself, 'I need to ask at least five questions in this conversation,' or 'I need to ask questions in this conversation, listen to the answers, and ask follow-up questions.' It's easy to do, and—even better—it requires almost no preparation." I go into the art of asking questions in more detail in chapter 14.

There is, however, a caveat: your questions should reflect a genuine interest in the person. If you're being overly nosy, you're likely to make the person you're speaking with feel uncomfortable, like they're in the firing line of your questions. It's about finding balance—and you do this by listening.

After learning about these studies, I had a conversation that required careful listening with a friend. My friend Margo had decided to retire, moving back to California from Oregon, where she had been living. When we met for lunch, she gave me her news and then told me that everyone was giving her unsolicited advice: *You need to follow a daily routine, you'll want to get a job or do volunteer work to get out of the house, you should join a book club or get involved in local politics,* and so on.

To me, this all sounded like so much opinion-noise. I asked her, "What do you want to do when you get back?"

Margo gazed into space for a moment, and then she said, "I really don't know yet."

So, I figured she really didn't know yet. I said, "Well, I guess that's what you'll do when you get back. Figure out who you want to be in the next phase of your life."

Margo smiled. "Yes," she said. Then she said, "You get it. That's what I want to do—take the time to figure out the next stage."

Listening is important, and follow-up questions matter. But, of course, friendship is about more than just our words. It's also about what we do.

TAKE ACTION

Samuel is the friend, mentioned earlier, who always fixed stuff for his friends. I used to go hiking and out to dinner with Samuel and his partner, whom I'd known first. Then they moved to Santa Barbara, and we didn't see much of each other. Until, that is, I was housesitting for the summer in Los Olivos, a small wine-tasting town near Santa Barbara. I invited Samuel's partner to a ladies-only evening of cooking, stargazing, movies—and it turned out that the uninvited Samuel saved my bacon.

I was fussing with my electric toothbrush, when two AA batteries popped out, rolled around the brightly tiled Moroccan sink, and gurgled down the plug hole. These batteries came to rest in the S-curve pipe under the sink, from where they would leak noxious acid into the septic tank—unless I got a high-priced plumber to fish them out. Said plumber was not in my budget. However, leaving the batteries to do their damage was not an option.

"Let's call Samuel," his partner suggested.

OK, so now Samuel is invited.

Samuel drove thirty miles with his plumbing tools in tow, and spent an hour fishing out the batteries and, as well, fixing a leak under the sink. All for a home-cooked chicken dinner.

Years later, when I started writing this book, I called Samuel to ask him why he loved being the fix-it guy for his friends. That's when he told me about the downside of always being *that* friend. He said that for years being the "helpful guy" was his coping strategy. He was good at fixing things, and he enjoyed helping other people—and then, he said, "I realized that I was trying to control how people saw me. I was being the helpful guy. I was fixing other people's issues, without fixing my own. And I expected friendship or love in return." We speak about this process in chapter 9, and here let's look at how Samuel eventually resolved this issue.

After some painful years while he came to this realization and learned how to shift his expectation, Samuel has come back to helping people—but now he helps people he truly likes. "I'm not looking for validation," he said. "I see being able to fix stuff as a gift, and now I really enjoy giving freely to people who I care about."

I was extremely grateful to Samuel for leaping into action when I needed his practical support. And I must say that this kind of active caring is the quintessential friendship: the person who helps us when we need that help.

Taking action has many forms. Most of us aren't particularly DIY or don't have computers to loan our friends. Other ways of stepping forward can be such simple acts as showing up when you say you will, putting your friend's preferences before your own on movie night, waiting to make sure your friend is safely in the door before driving off, letting go of the work that you did for their benefit. This last point may sound odd, but I have a particular story about this, and it has to do with this very book.

I actually started this book on friendship with my friend, Lisa Haisha. We were really on fire with our plan—and then she launched her own business and was rarely in town. That left me in a quandary about how to move this beloved project forward. So I wrote Lisa an email, discussing how I wanted to proceed with this book, asking for her ideas, and gently asking when she might have time for it. She wrote back immediately to thank me for the update, telling me to go ahead with it in my own way, and saying, "please feel free to use anything we worked on together"—meaning, she was letting go of her part of the project!

Now, that was an act of friendship!

And she didn't stop there. I'll talk about this in the next section.

EMPATHIZE ON ALL LEVELS

In chapter 8 we learn how we're hardwired to commiserate with a friend when they're down—when they haven't landed the job, the house, the romantic interest; when they've learned they have a tumor or they're grieving a loss. I've talked a lot about how important it is to be a good friend through another's difficulties. But there's something else, something related, that I've observed in my own life: it is vital to celebrate with our friends when they succeed.

My friend Lisa was very good about this—including me in her own successes and helping me to celebrate mine. This is a wonderful quality in a friend, and it's not always easy to do—because sometimes we're just not feeling celebrative when a friend leapfrogs (again!) up the corporate ladder. Or wins accolades in our own field of interest—whether it's in science, publishing, athletics, teaching, baking, or any of the arts. Or, their kid is just so successful at playing the violin, or graduated summa cum laude when our own child struggled to get Bs. These kinds of events may leave you grinding your teeth and saying, *Oh, yeah, I'm so happy for you.* Intellectually you know you should be happy for your friend, but emotionally you're just not feeling it. This has happened to me.

Many years ago, rather than sticking to a well-considered career path, I was traveling and investing a lot of my resources to research new ideas and learn more about my craft. At the time I sometimes felt iffy about this life plan of mine—especially when a friend I'd been to film school with wrote from Australia to say that she'd landed a producer's job on a movie. In other words, her career had jettisoned into the stratosphere! And here I was cleaning a rich woman's house for a few bucks an hour so that I could concentrate on a screenwriting course I was taking at a local college. While I was (yes, I really was!) very happy for my friend, learning about her success did cause me to take stock of my own life. Here I was, vacuuming a plush carpet in someone else's posh room and thinking, *Is this what I bargained for?* In this moment, I must admit, I felt a bit cheerless, so I get how tough it can be when you perceive that a friend has made the "right" choices necessary to find career success.

And feeling this way isn't only about celebrating their job or award successes either. It's all celebrations. Like my hairdresser who claimed she was oh-so-close with her friend. They had a loving, caring relationship. They adored each other. Until her friend got married and bought a house before she did either. These "successes" ignited a sense of competition inside my hairdresser—and, because she hadn't ever discussed what was going on for her, the issue remains unresolved. And it's quite likely their friendship isn't so "picture perfect" after all.

I read one academic paper on this topic that indicates the importance of being there for others when things are going right for them.[5] The study was based on seventy-nine dating couples, but I believe we can apply what was found to friendships as well. The higher participants rated their partners for having "active and constructive" responses to their successes, the closer they said they felt to that person and the less conflict they had in their relationship. An active-constructive response goes something like: *Congratulations, Kyle! You worked really long hours to get that project off the ground, and now your hard work has paid off. I'm happy you're being recognized.* The alternative responses to Kyle's big job success all sounded disparaging, dismissive, or something like, *Wow, you're going to have a tough time keeping up that momentum!*

It's sometimes easier to commiserate with a friend who's having difficulty because, in that case, you may feel superior to the friend—and your commiseration may leave them feeling inferior to you. The great benefit in acknowledging and praising a friend's accomplishments is that you can both experience positive emotions. And if you respond in "an active-constructive manner . . . these relationship resources, such as commitment, satisfaction, intimacy, and love, can be drawn on in the future."[6] (These are the kind of feelings we need to deepen our friendships.)

And in writing up the couples' study, the researchers note that "positive event disclosures offer all of the benefits that traditional social support exchanges confer without the same costs to self-esteem. . . . To put it colloquially, they seem to offer a lot more bang for the buck."[7]

This brings me to a situation that happened in my life years ago. I was taking a writing class at UCLA extension and was given an opportunity, along with my classmates and students from other writing classes, to submit a short story to a literary journal issued by the program. We all wanted to be among the ten authors whose stories would be published. After a few weeks our teacher announced the names of those accepted. My friend Nicole's name was on the list; mine wasn't. I felt both embarrassed and deflated—as if the wind had been knocked out of me.

Initially, I wasn't feeling much elation about Nicole's news. But, you know, I had a big talk with myself, and it helped me put this into perspective. Nicole is a gifted writer, and she had been working hard to continue growing in her art, to keep her writing fresh and current. Now, she was being given recognition that she deserved. So, with thoughts like this, I could let myself be delighted for my friend; I could congratulate her on her accomplishment. And, you know what? I really meant it!

Then I noticed that Nicole was being especially sensitive and generous toward me. Without diminishing her own excitement, she told me how much she liked my story and specifically what she liked about it. She said that this wasn't a judgment on the quality of my writing. Which it was—but, oh well. Nicole's support of me, her encouragement, felt lovely.

In an odd twist of fate, a week later the teacher announced that there was still room for one more story. It was between my story and one from another class. Yes, my story was selected. I was both surprised and happy, and so was Nicole. So we both got our stories published, *and* we strengthened our friendship!

• 13 •

Friends from a Distance

$\mathcal{F}$or most of us, sheltering in place through COVID-19 was an unprecedented experience, and many found it difficult to find our footing, let alone strengthen our ties—even though the latter would have helped us find our equilibrium. As if overnight, there were no more dinners out, book clubs, birthday parties, traveling, exercising together, going into the office or going out to a movie, no hugging, cheek kissing, hand holding, shoulder patting. What had seemed like normal activities came to a screeching halt. The pandemic was a dizzying life change for most of us.

And this all happened when I was about to wrap up this book, but then the pandemic struck and there was a whole new set of friend experiences to explore. One of the biggest challenges was "how do we strengthen our connections at a distance?" Some people found their friends to be a source of strength, while others may have found their friends to be unavailable, unsupportive, or even alienating.

My friend Chandra, who lives by herself, discovered just how crucial some of her friends were when, early in the pandemic, she fell sick with what she suspected was COVID-19. (There was no way for her to be tested at the time.) She could barely get out of bed, and several friends rallied by leaving healthy cooked food on her front porch, doing shopping for her, and keeping in regular contact by email. She was supremely grateful. She said, "For a few days, I was thinking, *Oh my God, this might be the end*. It wasn't, but I have to say that my friends really saved me." They were indispensable for her physical and emotional well-being.

On the other hand, many had experiences that left them feeling lonely and alienated—like Kurt, a dear friend from Boston who tested positive for COVID-19. His wife was hospitalized with the disease, and his father died due to complications from the virus. Kurt said his last goodbyes to his dad through the FaceTime app—a devastating experience. Once his quarantine was over, Kurt took a bicycle ride—*fresh air!*—around his wooded, sparsely populated suburb, but was confronted by a friend and neighbor who yelled, "Go home! I've got asthma; I have to stay alive for my kids. You shouldn't be getting close to people!" Kurt was stunned. He was riding about one hundred feet away from her, and was very likely in the antibody stage. He felt like a pariah.

So, the neighbor was having a heightened experience of fear, and Kurt had a heightened response as well: intense feelings of being shunned. In a situation like the pandemic, all our responses become amped up, our feelings heightened. Most of us were suddenly living digitally and with uncertainty—not knowing what was happening with the virus or food supplies, obsessing over toilet paper, scared about possibly being laid off, and, at the same time, not seeing many other people face to face. Remember, our brains don't deal well with change.

Our brains don't deal well with snubs, either. David T. Hsu, the psychiatry professor we met in chapter 5, explained to me that even virtual exclusion has a clearly measurable effect on the brain. "This is how a lot of these studies are currently being done," he said. "We're measuring virtual rejection. It's not like someone in the room is actually saying, *I don't like you; go away.* So, we know that virtual social rejection can be just as powerful as in-person rejection."[1]

To measure our responses to rejection, researchers often use an online ball-tossing game, Cyberball.[2] By manipulating how often the ball is tossed to someone, they can assess their response to social inclusion or ostracism. These games show much stronger responses when rejected, even if you just joined a digital ball game with a couple of avatars for a few minutes—which, when you think about it, is a pretty low bar.

That's why when we're operating online, at a distance, it's especially important to be transparent about our intentions and motivations with each other. During times of increased stress, it's worth being more mindful in our email messages, phone conversations, and now, with video conferencing—where people's faces are little pictures on a screen—because it's so easy for someone to misread our intent and meaning.

And then sometimes those digital full-face photos are large, especially at online parties—showing zits, frizzy hair, bad lighting, weird angle, or the virtual background of a Hawaiian beach that shimmies during the whole session. Then, there's the distracted person who mutes themselves so they can do other stuff online—*snurfing* rather than listening. The one who only talks about herself or hijacks the conversation. The one who is always late and joins the conversation with lot of fanfare—and so forth. Everything becomes more noticeable.

On the other hand, these observations can turn into benefits as well. I've heard from a few people who see the pandemic as a sort of wake-up call—a shaking of the friend tree, so to speak. Like what happened for me when I looked around the table at my Big Shift birthday party and suddenly realized, *These are not the people who are supporting my life.*

A FRIEND'S BEHAVIOR CLOSE-UP

Chandra developed a new approach to socializing while sheltering in place. She said, "The writing group I was in had devolved, over the years, into a wine-drinking group. In late March I started hosting a weekly happy hour get-together for this group on Zoom. Then, in April, I stopped drinking. The pandemic was beginning to feel like the end of the world was coming, and I didn't want to be heading into *that* getting my equanimity from wine." Chandra was worried at first that not drinking with her wine-swigging friends was going to be uncomfortable. "It didn't matter at all," she said. "And because the people in the group had been getting together on Zoom instead of in a local tavern, all of us are doing a lot more writing—which is wonderful because it's what we most love to share!"

Chandra added that she hasn't given up wine forever. "I did have a glass of wine last month," she said, "and I enjoyed it. But my habits have changed, and I think it's for the better. I like the interactions I'm having with people now." Even though in this time some of her friends fell away—she saw they didn't have enough in common—there were other friends she went on walks with (while social distancing) and that was a great way to keep up with the connections that most mattered to her.

Between letting go of wine and letting go of certain social connections, Chandra said that the pandemic became a time for her to reboot. "I began to feel stronger," she said, "and it was easier for me to stay in a positive frame of mind."

One of the ways that I can feel stronger is by acknowledging and overcoming a fear. When I experience anxiety, I tend to project my negative feelings onto either an object or another person. I speak about this tendency in chapter 7 in a falling-out I had with two friends over a cleaning deposit—my anxiety led me astray.

I've had this behavior from my childhood, and now—in my more conscious later years—I endeavor to find ways to offset these automatic reactions. Sometimes, however, my anxiety is either too new or too deep. In the instance I'm about to describe, I was clearly projecting my fears of catching the COVID-19 virus.

I meet with a group of people who I have considered associate friends; we share a common interest, although I haven't shared much personal information with them. However, I'd often see them when we were all attending scriptural seminars and lectures on theology at a monastery. Two in this extended group started having lunches with a group of women and invited me to join them, and eventually we switched to video conferencing to accommodate more people.

Then we came to the initial stages of the pandemic, when I began feeling a bit more anxious and uncertain. I started to wonder if I was contributing something worthwhile to this group. Other people would quote from spiritual philosophy; I most often spoke about the scientific research I was exploring for this book. I felt a bit like an outlier. This feeling of alienation grew to the point that I thought I may drop out. But then I remembered the rejection studies I had looked at and the interviews I had done on this subject. Hsu explained that "People who are more sensitive to social rejection will misinterpret others' intentions and perceive them as rejecting. Like, *so-and-so didn't add me to the email list; they must not really like me.*"

Was this what I was doing? I decided that I would consider the members of this group individually—look at each of them for what they had been giving me. In other words, I shifted my attention from myself to the other people. With that change in focus, I could see that one woman sent emails that were remarkably loving, sweet, and non-judgmental. Another woman, whom I had occasionally hung out with, showed her adorable little dog, giving me an oxytocin fix when I needed it. A new arrival revved me up with her energy. Another couple of women would listen quietly—and then surprise me with their thought-ful insights.

It was almost laughable what I'd projected onto these women, when I really thought about it. Like the time I felt as if I was rambling, one of the women said, "Oh, you mean such-and-such?" She had really heard me; she nailed what I was trying to express. And in another meet-ing, when I mentioned an online course I wanted to attend, someone in the group was enthusiastic about joining me in the course.

It's hard to believe that I could have left this virtual group that has been such a tremendous resource. I had to mentally get out of my own way to see that my own anxieties were creating the problems I thought I saw.

By taking another perspective on the situation, I offset my negative self-assessment; I went into what I see as "executive attention." This is when you shift your focus from your emotional mind into your thinking mind (frontal areas of brain, including anterior cingulate cortex). From the thinking mind, you can make clear decisions about the perceived issue at hand.

WAYS TO SHIFT YOUR ATTENTION

Raj Raghunathan, a marketing professor from the University of Texas who wrote a book on happiness, offered me some practi-cal tips to help calm down the brain from an emotional reac-tion into a more executive mindset. His example was this: say a colleague has sent you what you consider to be a terse and negative email or phone message. The first thing you should do, according to Raghunathan, is to recognize that you feel angry, confused, or upset. Then do one of these:

- Take the time to exercise or stretch so that you can get the anger and stress hormones out of your system. This reminded me of an experience I'd had once when a colleague berated me at the copy machine in front of others. I was so angry I couldn't think straight, so I went for a long speed walk outside. When I got back to the office, feeling refreshed, I encountered this person, who apologized profusely. I was in a mindset that I could accept his apology.
- If it's difficult to exercise, then watch a few cute clips online. And, yes, I'm talking about funny baby or puppy videos, because of the beneficent chemicals that are then released in your brain.
- Call a friend who always makes you laugh.

Once the emotional intensity has died down, you can read the email with less emotion, from a calmer state of mind. From this frame of mind—a more executive mode—you can then decide how to respond. You may choose to respond with a counterstrategy, or even find you agree with some of their points—even if you didn't appreciate the style of delivery. Or you may wish to ignore the message altogether. Attentional control helps you become more centered and take personal control.

NOTE

Raj Raghunathan (professor, marketing, McCombs School of Business, University of Texas), Skype interview with the author, May 2015.

PROS AND CONS OF DISTANCE FRIENDS

There are many conversations and studies on whether connecting through social media, Zoom conferencing, or live streaming strengthens or weakens our feelings of closeness and bonding with each other over time. My younger friends have adapted more easily to connecting electronically, whereas my older friends find this way of bonding to be shallow or unsustainable. My thought is that we, as a species, are in the first wave of this online media phenomena, so it's hard for us to see the long tail effects. Yet it's worth our taking a closer look.

First, let's set down some universal truths from research as well as anecdotes that I believe are independent of whether we live close to each other or connect through a digital medium. We experience rejection whether in the schoolyard or online; envy when competing with a work colleague whether it's in the office or on a post; jealousy if we see a friend flirting with our partner whether at a party or on a live stream; joyful when a friend wishes us a happy birthday on any medium; compassion if a friend has lost someone close to them; and shared amusement when we watch a puppy struggle to get into an oversized box—whether virtual or not.

It's amazing just how much we exchange in real time from afar. I can be walking on a California hiking trail while talking to my sister who is doing a load of laundry in Queensland, Australia. Unlike our forebears a dozen generations back, we no longer have to spend months traveling across deserts, oceans, or mountains to see each other or in waiting for a letter to arrive.

On the other hand, I have to wonder if our brains, with our tribal thinking, have adapted to these digital experiences.

Robin I. M. Dunbar, professor emeritus in experimental psychology at the Magdalen College, Oxford, is the researcher who formulated the Dunbar number: "A measurement of the cognitive limit [150] to the number of individuals with whom any one person can maintain stable relationships."[3] There are many theories about whether or not we can maintain healthy communities online, and in a 2015 study conducted by Dunbar, he concludes,

> The data shows that the size and range of online egocentric social networks, indexed as the number of Facebook friends, is similar to that of offline face-to-face networks. For one sample, respondents also specified the number of individuals in the inner layers of their network (formally identified as support clique and sympathy group), and these were also similar in size to those observed in offline networks. This suggests that, as originally proposed by the social brain hypothesis, there is a cognitive constraint on the size of social networks that even the communication advantages of online media are unable to overcome.[4]

So, our brain still has the same cognitive constraints with our circle of friends—*clique and sympathy group*—whether we connect face to face or online. Many of the high numbers we see on social media, Dunbar surmises, could be considered "promiscuous friending" of individuals who have tenuous links to one another. (As Dunbar points out, some Facebook friends are actually friends of a friend of a friend.)[5] This is what in my own media days I would have called *promotional hype*.

And there are social scientists who posit that these online connections are having a negative net effect on friendship, saying that through our consistent use of technology, we're losing the art of conversation. Sherry Turkle, professor in the program on Science, Technology and Society at Massachusetts Institute of Technology, raises an alarm about how increasingly distracted we have now become in our face-to-face interactions because of digital technology. Turkle says, "I am not anti-technology, I am pro-conversation." Speaking in an interview with *The Guardian* in 2015, she cites the statistic that "89% of Americans admit they took out a phone at their last social encounter—and 82% say that they felt the conversation deteriorated after they did so." She adds, "It is captured by the story I tell of the young girl saying: 'Daddy! Stop Googling! I want to talk to you.'"[6]

On the other hand, Dunbar also observes that teenagers "have much smaller offline social networks than adults . . . and forcing them to enlarge their network with large numbers of anonymous 'friends-of-friends' may place significant strain on their ability to manage their networks."[7] By keeping these smaller groups, young people can maintain their closer ties through these smaller, more private groups, keeping their "cognitive limit" intact. Even so, Dunbar notes, "In practical terms, it may reflect the fact that real (as opposed to casual) relationships require at least occasional face-to-face interaction to maintain them."[8]

I believe that most relationships, at any level, need some face-to-face interaction. Only then can we truly read another person's body language, manner, and responses to their environment.

More than a decade ago, a colleague and I worked together by phone and through email, without ever meeting in person. Our project went sour, and when that happened, we had no personal juice to resolve the issues at hand—no relational resilience. We hadn't shared a laugh over flavored coffees at a cafe or exchanged winks over a private joke in the office kitchen. In my experience, we get a tremendous amount of information from body language, by observing a person's response to the environment—remember, we have five (possibly more) senses, not just two.

Now, when we become bored, we seek out our devices. Even when we're talking with someone face to face, we might "phub" it—that is, ignore the social situation we're in and engage instead with our mobile device. Turkle writes, "It all adds up to a flight from conversation—at least from conversation that is open-ended and spontaneous, conversation in which we play with ideas, in which we allow ourselves to be fully present and vulnerable. Yet these are the conversations where empathy and intimacy flourish and social action gains strength. These are the conversations in which the creative collaborations of education and business thrive."[9]

In other words, sometimes we just have to be in the same space to resolve an issue. During the time I worked for the newspaper in Santa Barbara, the paper moved offices, and I threw out a lot of paperwork. A few weeks later, a man who had entrusted me with his poem collection for possible publication—a man who was living on the streets—showed up at our new location, asking for the writing he'd left with me. To my horror, I realized I had mistakenly discarded it before the move. I felt terrible, but he felt a lot worse and was furious with me—*rightly so!*—because this was the only copy of his writing that he had. I could sense the pain rising within him, and I felt an overwhelming sadness for my thoughtless action. What I had done was indefensible. I'd really screwed up. And I spent a long time talking with this man, conveying my sincere regret, and asking for his forgiveness. Slowly, he calmed down. He could see that this was truly a mistake on my part and that it hadn't happened because I'd marginalized either him or his work. We parted company on reasonable terms.

I am sure that this very raw exchange that led to a healing between two people could never have happened online, whether it was via conferencing or phone, streaming or email. This man and I had to be together, in a shared physical space, eye to eye, in order to come to that heart-to-heart connection.

As Dunbar notes in another study, "Reading others' faces—impossible during a conventional phone call—may be an evolutionarily conserved means for exchanging pivotal information. . . . Faces offer a plethora of social information about the sex, age, ethnicity, and emotional expressions of an individual, and potentially about their intentions and mental state (all of which influence the strength of the bond between two individuals)."[10]

I personally do not think that as human beings we have evolved and acculturated ourselves to that level of bonding online—yet.

My close connections—most of them now quite far-flung—began in physical proximity. I experienced whether this person is cranky or happy in the morning, whether they're messy or neat, whether they smell soapy clean or slightly feral, whether or not they like hugging, and, most importantly, whether they make a good cup of tea. The kind of information you wouldn't post on a dating app or roommate ad, but small observations, small gestures, which all add up.

Then, once we have created a bond with each other, the question is how can we maintain our friendship from afar.

An article I read outlined how important it is to set a new foundation for newly long-distance friendships—and not depend on reliving memories of shared experiences or bringing this person into the daily minutiae of your new life. April Bleske-Rechek, a psychology professor at the University of Wisconsin, explains, "Whether your relationship was more about talking or doing, your best bet is to just adapt that core element to your new circumstances."[11]

Ways to stay connected could include finding activities you can both enjoy long-distance—such as launching a book club together through visual conferencing. Or include your friends in a current project by asking their opinion, like I did with my friends when I needed help picking out a design for the cover of this book.

And I can add another way to keep these vital connections active in our life, after a discussion I had with my friend Nora on this topic.

MOVING FORWARD WHILE CONNECTING FROM AFAR

Recently, I talked to Nora about why we've been engaged in each other's lives for such a long time. Nora and I live some distance from each other, and neither one of us lives near our dearest friends. She replied that long-distance friendship can be a little like a romance in that you can focus on ideas and connections, rather than looking for curtains together—although we've probably done that at some time. What I think she meant is that you can find creative ways to integrate these long-distance friends into your life. When Nora sees something, she may think, *Glenda would love that!* And I do that as well. When I hear a motivational speaker, I may think, *I'll share that with Nora and Lisa.* When I find a fun food website, I think of Ava. Or if I haven't heard from Jessica or Nicole or Paula, I'll think, *It's time to check in.*

It's as if we hold all of our close friends in a mental landscape, so we can interact with them in absentia. I wonder if this is a primitive instinct, to keep our distant, deep connections alive. I saw a documentary about a family of elephants, each of whom recognized the others at a rescue facility where they had been brought together from different circuses. These elephants were trumpeting and bashing the walls, they were so excited to see each other again. It was one of the most moving moments I've ever seen on television. In the same way, I think our friends become part of our mental landscape.

So, we can continue friendships at a distance, even though our time of bonding usually begins in a shared physical space—we hug and hang out and learn each other's spontaneous response expressions.

As we discussed in chapter 1, it's important to be aware of the qualities and goals we share with our friends—and this is true whether those friends are living halfway across the planet or in the same house with us. Be responsive to each other as well. Return calls, texts, and emails promptly, so the person feels respected and heard.

Yet I also think there may be something more to it than that.

Amelia was the first real friend I made in the United States. She invited me to her home outside San Francisco for the holidays, where her mom introduced me to strong sherbet cocktails and her dad explained the Super Bowl to me. Amelia and I have felt bonded ever since, although we lived in the same town for only a year. Amelia has been a witness to most of my adult history—even though it's mostly from a distance—and I have been that for her as well.

Recently, I reminded her about the time I was working for a weekly newspaper in Santa Barbara, and she was a publicist in Los Angeles. This was pre-digital, and every week I'd have to drive the paper's galleys to LA and then drive home again. One week as I was driving back home on the 101, I thought of Amelia: *I haven't seen her for a while. Maybe I'll drop by.* I was getting close to the exit for Amelia's house, going back and forth in my mind. *Yes, I haven't seen her in months* was warring with *No, I've got a full day tomorrow.* Then, suddenly, I decided *yes*, took the exit, and pulled over to call her from a pay phone. (This was also before cell phones.)

As soon as Amelia heard my voice on the phone she laughed. "I can't believe you're calling me right now!" She explained that she had just gotten down the salad bowl I'd given her as a wedding gift, and was asking herself whether to use it that evening: *yes? no?*

So, the answer to both our questions was *yes*.

Some experiences with friends and family defy explanation. And my intuition tells me that this is true for many people. Even if you're someone who doesn't think in terms of intuition, I wonder if you don't have a deeply personal sharing with some of your friends. Something you have with this person and nobody else. Something you can't quite pinpoint, yet you recognize that it's there.

And sometimes this relational sauce doesn't need a lot of time to heat up in the personal space either. Amelia made friends with someone she met on a cruise and now, even though she hasn't spent a lot of time with this person, she considers her an essential friend. They're successfully hanging out long distance—from San Francisco to London.

The issue this raises is significant to many of us in this modern world: connecting with friends over physical distance. In chapter 15, I discuss moving through personal, social, and cultural distances as well.

MAINTAINING NEW FRIENDS LONG DISTANCE

Amelia had accompanied her mother on a cruise between Amsterdam and Budapest, and she made a new friend, Nell, on their day trip to Cologne. It was her mother, Rita, who introduced the other two women. They became inseparable, the three musketeers, for the next twelve days—the rest of the cruise. The three of them laughed a lot; they chatted and shopped. And five years later, they were still close, which surprised Nell, who told Amelia that she didn't think she needed any new friends. Until, that is, she met Amelia and Rita.

And Amelia had pretty much the same feeling. She had plenty of friends in her life. She wasn't looking for a new friend on this cruise; she was hoping to spend some time with her mom. One of the things Amelia liked so much about Nell was the way she got along with Amelia's mother. "She loved my mother desperately, and my mom could be hard person to take. She's got a very tough personality. But she's very true to herself, and Nell has that quality as well."

Nell visited Amelia and Rita in California, and Amelia visited Nell in London. They had planned their next cruise together for September 2020: from Prague to Berlin.

But at the beginning of the COVID-19 pandemic, Rita learned that she had cancer and that the disease had spread throughout her body. Amelia then moved her mother into a residential care facility. When

Nell found out, she wanted to see Rita. Amelia told her that Rita was failing rapidly. This conversation happened on a Friday, and that day Nell booked a flight for the next Monday. The pandemic complicated travel, however, and by Saturday, the U.S. government had banned flights from Europe—which meant that Nell would have been in quarantine for fourteen days after her arrival. Amelia said, "We both agreed she had to cancel."

The three musketeers were able to connect one last time through a video conferencing app. "Mom and Nell had the chance to share their feelings," Amelia said. Each of the women could tell the other how much she loved her and how much their friendship had meant to her. "It was beautiful and heartbreaking," Amelia said. "Mom made Nell promise to go on the cruise with me and spread some of her ashes while toasting 'the Old Gal.'"

Amelia and Nell have scheduled a cruise from Rome to Greece in 2022, in honor of Rita, and will spread her ashes—along with Amelia's father's ashes—in the Strait of Messina by Sicily, their ancestral home.

Reaching out to new people can effectually expand your personal borders. In the next chapter we discuss ways to make this process happen more smoothly.

• 14 •

Being Open to Making New Friends

$\mathcal{M}$y husband is the retiring sort, so when he took my car in to be smog-checked on his way to work one morning and was sent to cool his heels in the auto shop waiting room, he only acknowledged the other person there with a brief nod. Then John noticed that the middle-aged woman, gazing at her phone, was wearing a T-shirt with the word "mindfulness" written across the top with a little Asian signature symbol he recognized. He asked her, "Is that Thich Nhat Hanh's symbol on your shirt?" Thich Nhat Hanh is a Buddhist monk from Vietnam, a worldwide peace activist and someone for whom John has great respect.

"Why yes, it is," the woman said, looking up.

John asked if she'd been to any of Hanh's lectures. She said no, but she liked his philosophy—and then John was able to tell her that he and I had seen Thich Nhat Hanh in Pasadena a few years back.

Before long, the two of them had introduced themselves—her name is Leanne—and she was telling John that on this particular morning she'd just "grabbed any shirt out of the closet" when she was getting dressed—and this, as John put it, launched a "discussion that went from zero to a hundred in just ten minutes."

Telling me about the experience the following day, John said, "It's rare I feel motivated to make small talk. Usually, I feel like the fly on the wall." He pointed out then that a close friend (Gavin) and his wife (me) are both voluble talkers, and John is usually the one who listens. "I have this myth about myself that I'm not really interested in people," he said. "I'm the withdrawn guy who sits in corners and plays with computers."

That morning in the mechanic's waiting room, John saw something about this stranger that sparked his interest—he saw the possibility of making an authentic connection with someone he hadn't yet met. His spontaneous question launched an exploration. "I almost felt as if I became a bon vivant," John told me the next day, "just like Gormley." Gormley is a vivacious friend of ours, a kind of gold standard for conversational ease.

A few days before John's encounter with Leanne, he and I had talked in some detail about the Harvard study I cited in chapter 12. This study evaluating the importance of asking follow-up questions in a conversation had found that asking follow-up questions increases your likability when you're making new contacts. John wasn't consciously applying this principle that morning in the waiting room, but I wonder if it didn't influence him all the same. The study was quite specific in ways I didn't go into in that chapter. I think it's worth looking at these in greater detail now.

IMPLEMENTING FOLLOW-UP QUESTIONS

John is an engineer and likes specific directions, so that's why he was especially interested in the way this study went into various types of questions. The most basic was identified simply as a *follow-up*—although, of course, they were all ways of following up. But the direct "follow-up" question was one that asked, simply, for more information about what the person had said.

One example of a follow-up is when John mentioned to Leanne that he'd seen Thich Nhat Hahn in Pasadena; Leanne asked him, "How did you feel when you saw him?" She was asking for more information about what John had just told her. As the study notes, "Follow-up questions reflect general-inquiry questions that begin with *why* or *how*, which request that the other person provide information."[1] This is the most popular kind of question to receive. People who are asked for more information know that you're taking in what they're telling you—*and* that you're interested enough to want to know more.

Another type of response is what the study's authors called a *full-switch*. These are questions about a new topic, one unrelated to what the other person has already mentioned. Continuing with our example, when John mentioned to Leanne that he and I had gone to see Thich Nhat Hahn in Pasadena, she might have replied, "Do you and your wife eat out much in Orange County?" That would be a turnaround in the topic—and it's understandably the least popular form of follow-up question.

Another form is a *partial switch*, which changes the topic a bit but not entirely. Instead of asking about restaurants in the example above, Leanne might have asked about other lectures John and I had been to— which would be related but not on John's topic.

Finally, there is a *mirror question*, which is to reply to a question with the identical question. If John had asked Leanne "Would you ever go to Pasadena to hear Hanh speak?" and Leanne replied, "I'd love to see him speak. Would you go see him again?" this would be a mirror.

The study's authors write, "We find that responsiveness was higher among people who asked more follow-up questions and lower among people who asked more full-switch questions. We also find that follow-up questions alone predicted increased partner liking."

So, the idea of follow-up questions and likability was fresh in John's mind when he walked into that waiting room. It was a good experience for him, and he wants to be sure that it doesn't end there. The way he put it was this: "How can I leverage this newfound skill, rather than putting it back into the closet?"

A few weeks after this mechanic's waiting room encounter, John and I were leaving for an extended stay in Australia to visit family and old friends. The first time we visited Australia together was years ago, and John was—well, let's say that he wasn't putting himself forward. One evening in Melbourne, we spent the evening with some of my close college friends. While the rest of us laughed and chatted around the dining table, John spent a lot of the night in the next room, fixing our host's computer networking system. This was John's preference—even his idea!—and while it helped out my friend, it didn't allow John to get to know any of these people.

At the end of our mini–Melbourne tour, one Aussie friend observed that John didn't talk much. Putting a positive spin on it, she mused, "Well, I guess someone has to listen."

On our recent trip to Australia, John had gone there to work, so it wasn't a huge social experience for him. But I saw him deeply engaged in talking to new people at parties, and he arranged to go on outings with his colleagues without me.

He ever-so-slightly shifted his mindset. This is not an easy thing to do, and John knows there is more for him to work on. It's a process.

PRACTICE CONNECTING WITH OTHERS

So, how can we walk with ease into a totally new, uncomfortable environment? There's a lot of fear around this situation. When I spoke with Barry Collodi,[2] the executive coach featured in chapter 11, he mentioned that he has developed practicums to help people change some of their mental habits. Such training can show someone who's shy how to deliver an engaging Power Point presentation or walk confidently into a room full of strangers.

"I do presentation skills training," Collodi said, "and I work a lot with twenty-somethings, both men and women. Everyone hates presenting; it's everyone's biggest fear. So, people get very shy and very quiet, and they say nothing." Collodi videos these groups and lets the participants watch themselves afterward, giving everyone the opportunity to see their own awkwardness.

"Then, I say 'Come here, Glenda. Here's what we're going to do. You're no longer going to be Glenda, aged twenty-three; you're Bianca, my boss. You hired me six weeks ago, you relocated me to New York, and I don't know anybody here. It's Friday night, you're giving a party with thirty to forty people in your apartment, and you've invited me— very kindly—to meet people. So, I'm going to knock at the door, and you be Bianca and let me in.'"

Suddenly the entire premise is different. Now, the person Collodi is working with stands before him with a big smile on their face. The person says, "Come in! I'm so glad you're here," And they usher him into the space with a welcoming gesture.

"They have changed completely," Collodi said. "And I let them see this on the video. I tell them, 'Understand, when you're greeting another person, always think of yourself as the host or hostess at a party. Invite them to enjoy their time with you.'"

I loved his example. It's about giving yourself the power and credibility to inhabit the space you're in, to own it. This can be difficult to do because, as Collodi pointed out, we all have some level of anxiety. To become more self-assured it's important to do what you'd do when taking on any new skill: to practice.

You'd have to practice anything else, right? If you discovered you were a naturally talented athlete or musician or writer, you'd still have to practice! So, the same is true for your social skills.

And now there has been an exponential growth in technology tracking what's going on inside the brain through functional magnetic resonance imaging—a noninvasive brain imaging technique—whereby we can visualize the brain's response to anxiety and fear.

Some of the experiments used by scientists such as Jason Moser—the psychology professor we heard from in chapter 9—look at techniques such as "third-person self-talk," which is a way to distance yourself from anxious thoughts.[3] Third-person self-talk is quite literally that: you give yourself a silent pep-talk: *Glenda is pretty nervous about this evening*. Once you practice self-talk, you can start reinterpreting these talks in a positive light: *I know you're pretty nervous about this evening, Glenda, but just put on your lucky dress and best smile, and you'll be fine!*

And let me say that even though I consider myself open socially, there have been a number of times when I've walked into a big fancy event with wildly successful people and have suddenly become shy, potentially mute. What on earth do I have to offer this award winner, or that popular and sophisticated luminary? That's when I decided to become the character I wanted to be—the very best I have to offer.

We all have something great to offer. Third-person speak is one way of accessing this "something great." When we employ this strategy, shifting in this way from first to third person, there is a corresponding shift in the brain: we move out of the amygdala (our seat of fear) and closer to the cerebral cortex (our center of thought). So, by taking ourselves out of first-person identification with a scene, we move away from our emotional intensity. By speaking to ourselves in the third person, we become clearer and better able to perform. This simple language switch makes us less likely to ruminate on our fears and more likely to focus on the situation at hand. It gives us a better perspective on what's happening.[4]

This has been tested many times. Moser had this to say about third-person speak when I talked to him: "We found, across behavioral studies and two neural imaging studies, that just talking to yourself in the third person gives you a bit of psychological distance from negative experiences. It allows you to look at it almost as if it had happened to somebody else. It's almost as if you'd given advice to somebody else."[5]

Moser described how in one study he and his cohorts told one group of subjects to use first-person pronouns: *I'm really stressed out. I think I'm going to fail. I think they're going to judge me.* At the same time, the researchers instructed the other group to speak about their feelings in the third person: *Jason is really scared that people are going to judge him. Patty is terrified about giving this speech.*

Just this small linguistic shift was enough to make a difference. Moser said, "We found that just switching the speech to that third-person language quieted down the emotional brain as well as improved people's performance in these social interactions."[6]

I did something like this years ago when a friend asked me to read a short poem at her wedding, which was quite the social occasion and was attended by a number of Big Names. At first, I felt anxious. I had been handed the poem—a very *short* poem—but I felt there was no way I could stand up and read even a short poem in front of this crowd! Then I adopted the attitude that I was an actor, Glenda, reading a line for the bride and groom in a play. Playing the part of Glenda flipped the switch for me, just like third-person speak does. I distanced myself from the whole thing by seeing myself as someone else who was *acting* a part, and in that way, I shifted out of my nervousness.

It worked. The reading went just fine. So, over the years I've taken on what I call my Glenda persona and, most of the time, she has helped me approach intimidating people or dive into scary situations with more confidence.

Whether we use third-person speak or Collodi's practice of assuming the role of host, these methods are effective ways to step past the fears we might associate with our own, everyday persona. The need for such a ploy is not unusual when you're meeting new people or encountering a group of people.

THE POWER IN DIVERSITY

When we talk about our reticence to approach somebody new, the first thing that comes to mind is shyness. However, I believe some of our reticence may be about finding it difficult to approach a person who doesn't look, act, or sound like us.

A person may dress more flamboyantly. She may be from a different race, background, or culture. He may be gay—or straight. She might be much older—or much younger. Or perhaps we feel some awkwardness around a person's disability. Yet the beauty and nature of friendship is that our friends can be anyone from whom we can learn, anyone who can help us grow. This means they don't have to look like a member of our family. Through our friends, we can explore our independent selves.

MAKING NEW FRIENDS

We've learned many practical techniques on how to improve our communication skills, from asking follow-up questions to taking on the role of host during a networking event to quell your anxiety when meeting new people. However, I want to bring up a whole new way of finding and making new friends. When we're younger our friends are colleagues, other parents, or neighbors, but it's important to learn to find friends who feed your independent self as well. So, at any age, rather than looking for friends, start figuring out your own passion, what interests you, and pinpoint what dreams you have or adventures you want to pursue. It's about finding people who naturally share your interests.

Here are some suggestions to get started:

- *What are three things you love to do?* For example, creating art, going on hikes, or reading. Then, take a class, volunteer at a community center, or clean up hiking trails. Find people who are indigenous to your own inclinations.
- *What is your dream adventure?* For example, travel to Italy, learn to make chocolate, perform in a local play. So, you could learn Italian, find a dessert class, or volunteer at the local theater company. This exposes you to people who share the same dreams and sense of adventure.
- *What are ways you are likely to stay healthy?* For example, biking, dancing, or your favorite way to keep your brain active—attending library events or college lectures. I met my friend who convinced me to stay in the United States when we were both walking to the same lecture.

As a next step, when you feel you connect with someone who shares your interests and passion, invite them out for coffee or a drink. And regardless of the outcome—whether or not you get closer—enjoy this time together.

Find out what you love to do, and the friends will follow.

What I mean by *independent selves* is that we're free to consider friendships with people who help us express new and varied sides of our personalities—people with whom we might have to reach to find mutual understanding and common interests and goals. We may not have a shared history or DNA with these people, but we're attracted to their character and behavior. Because friendships are voluntary, we can have multiple friends, and we can choose our level of commitment to each friend. That gives us a lot of room for freedom of expression in friendship.

What many of us do, however, is bring our biases into our friendships, choosing only the friends who feel comfortable and reflect our familial ties. This came up in a recent conversation I had with my friend Paula, a New York producer who is originally from Jamaica. She was telling me about a gourmet food tour in Italy she'd been on with our mutual friend Ava—and it sounded like so much fun! Among other things, the tour group met chefs at various *trattorias* (family restaurants) and learned how to make the four Roman sauces from scratch. Paula told me that the host of the tour, who was Jewish, was amazed that Paula, who has no Jewish ties, was interested in a trip to Italy that focused on Jewish cuisine.

"Why wouldn't I be interested?" Paula asked her. "I'm curious, I'm open to learn about another culture, and I love it when someone is interested to learn about mine."

During this same trip, the host also commented to Paula that she'd never had a black friend. This didn't surprise Paula. "Actually," Paula said. "I'm more surprised to find white people who have diversity in their group." That's when Paula referred to our friend Ava, who is white. "I see how Ava's really interested in other cultures. She embraces a person, regardless of their race. And if she sees a lack of diversity she'll speak up. Race doesn't define her."

I'd met Paula through Ava, and Paula told me that Ava is one of the few white women she's met who truly relates to her with equanimity, and without bias or discomfort. So, when Paula invited Ava on a scuba trip to Central America with a predominantly African American dive group, she knew Ava would be completely comfortable. Ava was delighted to join in. For her, it was "Terrific! Let's go!"

I had my own *terrific, let's go* experience last year on a tour in South China. John and I took a cruise past the jagged limestone hills along the scenic Li River from Guilin to Yangshuo. When we got off the ferry, our tour guide took us to a small farming community, and there, quite by accident, we stumbled upon a traditional Chinese house that had been turned into a modern boutique hotel. From the inner courtyard, a cool, thirty-something Chinese dude, sporting a porkpie hat and goatee, invited us to join a small gathering of his friends. Three women in their late twenties or early thirties were sitting by a fireplace inside a cozy, charmingly decorated, pine-beamed apartment.

John and I sat down, and shortly we were drinking tea and eating roast yams hot off the coals while we chatted with the others through our guide. Two more women arrived, one carrying a guitar. It was a few weeks before Christmas, so it was the most natural thing in the world to sing some carols. We started with "Jingle Bells" and "Santa Claus Is Coming to Town" in English, and then the guitarist sang in Mandarin, both carols and some traditional Chinese songs.

Our new friend in the hat left for a bit and then reappeared lugging a six-foot Christmas tree. When he plugged in the tree, sparkling blue lights lit up the whole room. The ambience was enchanting—a truly memorable afternoon.

This was a group of people I could easily hang with in California—welcoming, fun, open, curious. We didn't even speak the same language, but we had no trouble communicating. It felt as if this beautiful, airy room was the most natural destination for us, and the people we met there were like an extension of our own group of friends.

This experience let me know that commonality doesn't have to be defined by race, culture, gender, background, someone's disability, or even language; it doesn't depend on what's familiar to us. It's as if we've tricked ourselves into seeing the differences in others, and we forget that people are, ultimately, human beings, just like us. When we make a connection with someone, what we're really connecting with is that person's character. The beauty of friendship is that we don't have to be tied to tradition or family concepts about who we are—we can explore relationships outside this mindset.

And that's when we realize how greatly rewarding it can be to reach out.

Beyond Proximity

$\mathscr{I}$ opened this book by talking about my Big Shift birthday party—the moment I saw that the people celebrating with me were not the people who energized or encouraged me in life. From the outside, we probably looked like we were having fun together, but inside I felt lonely.

It took time for me to understand what was really happening at that party. Later, when I contemplated this, I saw that I was spending most of my time with the people who were easiest to connect with—familiar people, people who lived nearby or who worked with me. At the same time, I had other friends I adored, and these were the friends with whom I shared my life's goals, the friends who helped me to achieve those goals.

Somehow, I'd confused proximity, physical closeness, with esteem and essence—which is another level of friendship altogether. Clearly, we need access to someone so that we can get to know them. However, as one of my dear friends who was not at that particular birthday party later observed, "I think a lot of friendships happen because of proximity. I have friends around here. I have a girlfriend I go walking with in the morning. I have a girlfriend who lives behind me—she runs a pizza parlor with her partner. Occasionally we get together; we all sit out by her pool. They have a boat, and we go out boating with them. But we get together because of proximity. She's fine, I like her, and she's a fun neighbor to do things with. But I know if she moved today, we probably wouldn't keep in touch."

These are the friends whom I describe as collaborators (friends who offer immediate emotional support and continuity) or associates (people with whom we share a common interest). There are also those casual friends in your extended circle who you barely know yet can also offer you opportunities—if sought.[1] Mark Granovetter, a Stanford sociology professor who has done research on social contacts, calls these lower-stake connections *weak ties*.[2] He found that our weak ties can be highly beneficial for professional networking and job opportunities. Since then other researchers have established that these casual relational links can make a surprising contribution to a person's sense of well-being—can give a person a greater sense of belonging in the community.[3] And I can see this in my own life, chatting with my hairdressers, other adult ed students, the fitness wannabes I gab with before the beginning of exercise classes, the next-door neighbor who shares household tips gives me a great sense of connectedness.

It's great to enjoy these weak ties for the social connections they are. The danger comes, I feel, when we confuse them for something that's more enduring.

Even though proximity is, in itself, a pretty feeble basis for attraction—why Granovetter calls it a *weak tie*—it does, in and of itself, affect how we see people. Research studies have shown that people may feel close to someone they have never spoken to simply because they live near them in an apartment building or attend the same class.[4]

One such study focused on graduate students living in the same housing facility, and found that the subjects felt closer to students who lived next to the mailboxes or near a stairwell than to those living on an upper floor. The subjects felt closest to the people they saw more often, even though they didn't know them any better. Scott Eidelman, the professor who discussed transitions in chapter 7, observed, "The more you see someone, the closer you are to them, the more you like them. So, this is another reason why people seem to like what they're familiar with—it's this idea of mere exposure."

Eidelman brought up another study that makes an even stronger point about the mere-exposure effect.[5] In this second study, four female students "of similar appearance" were asked to join a large university class of about five hundred students. Three of the four look-alike women were asked to sit in the front row of the lecture hall, saying nothing to anyone else in the class. One of these women attended all fifteen sessions; the second woman attended ten sessions; the third only five sessions; and the fourth did not attend any sessions.

On the final day of class, the researcher projected photographs of all four women onto a screen at the front of the classroom and asked the students to, as Eidelman put it, "make some judgments about the pictures: *How attractive is this person? How similar are they to you? To what extent do you think you would be friends?* These sorts of things.

"What the researcher found is the more often the woman came to class, the more you like this person, the more attractive you think they are, the more likely you are to think they're similar to you, the more likely you are to think you would be friends."

Remember, these four women didn't speak to anyone while attending these lectures—they came in, sat down, packed up, and left. It was merely their exposure to others that determined how these others rated the women's attractiveness and likability.

I would say that when mere exposure is the basis of friendly feelings, then there's a certain interchangeability to these relationships. It's this sense of interchangeability, I find, that can lead to deep feelings of loneliness. In chapter 1, we discussed the devastating effects loneliness has on our health. In one study, it's been reported that since the 1980s, when we had at least three confidantes, we now—thirty years later—have fewer than one.[6] And possibly an even bigger shift in Western society is that more people are living alone than ever before.

"This amazing thing starts to happen in the early twentieth century and to really take off in the 1950s," sociology professor Eric Klinenberg says in a radio interview, "which is that for the first time in the history of our species, people start to settle down on their own and to live alone for long periods of time."[7]

That is a huge shift!

Yet living alone is different from feeling lonely. In fact, Klinenberg went on to say that many people who live alone are highly social; and many people living with others can feel lonely. Even though this may be so, I wonder how people who live alone (and who are highly social) have been affected by sheltering in place during the pandemic.[8] This is when essential friends become more important. I'm talking about the kind of friends who will set up a protocol to check in with you during a big event: birth, death, fire, flood, or pandemic. The kind of friends who are not interchangeable, and who are part of your mental landscape. The people who, over time, you have learned to love. Remember, the root word for "friend" is "love."

So, that's why it's important to make friendship connections that are not interchangeable.

FOCUSING ON LONG-TERM CONNECTIONS

Recently Mr. Late, from the Big Shift birthday party, visited Los Angeles from the East Coast. He texted, "Yes, really want to visit. Looking forward to seeing you!" I invited him to stay with us in Orange County, but said that if he didn't have wheels, I'd meet him in Los Angeles—I was flexible. We'd talked occasionally on the phone, but we hadn't seen each other in well over eight years. I wanted to discuss this book with him and to hear about his current projects. I called and texted him to make plans, yet he only left me one quick phone message. After that, when I texted, he'd text back the equivalent of a "thumbs-up" emoji with no specifics. So, not surprisingly, we didn't get together. Initially, I admit, I felt hurt and perplexed. Then I stopped to reflect on how easy it was for our old familiar pattern to emerge—me expecting something from him and then feeling that he'd let me down.

Once I felt free from my expectations—we'd either meet or we wouldn't—I no longer dwelled on the situation. I focused on what I had learned from this book. I had a toolkit now. I focused on what rejection really is. I realized there is no threat there. The threat of rejection is only imaginary.

Then I systematically worked through my process, which started with these questions:

- What am I looking for in a friend?
- What are my long-term interests?
- What are five character traits I most look for in a person?

- Is there someone I really admire and what are the qualities that person has?
- Who can I see myself going on a trip with in five years' time?

I arrived at my friendship system from these questions. I started by writing down a list of all my friends: from the ones I'd seen in the last six months to some I hadn't seen in two or three years. Next to each friend's name, I wrote down five words that described their qualities. Remember the qualities I came to that I was looking for in a friend: *curious, visionary, encouraging, enterprising, purposeful.* These were the qualities I wanted to attract into my life. And that's when I saw *the* five friends, the ones who popped out to me—the ones who had the qualities I wanted to attract into my life. And guess what? Not one of them had been at that birthday party. Why not? I hadn't invited them.

This is when I saw how I'd been spending most of my quality time with people who were physically close, who were easily accessible. And, interestingly, these were the friends who slowly dropped away from my life after we stopped working together, and after I met the person I would marry. It was during this transitional period when I started to pay attention to what I wanted in my future, including those friends who would support and energize me. Jessica was one, Lisa another—even though we'd been friends for just a few years, we'd invested time and energy into keeping our connection alive. They lived in town, and the others on my new "connection list" lived out of town. These became my foundational friendships, the ones I've been calling my essential friends.

Now, I have to confess that when I think back to the people who were at that all-important Big Shift birthday party, there is only one I'm still seeing—and that's just occasionally, when he's in town. I don't feel unfriendly toward any of these old buddies; in fact, I'm still quite fond of a few of them. Yet, we rarely text or email each other anymore.

The irony here is that there may be someone right there in your peripheral vision who you don't initially realize could turn into an essential friend. That's what I've found. Then, through various circumstances you stay in touch, possibly either one or the other reaches out, and a stronger relationship begins. Here's an example.

When I was working for a newspaper in Santa Barbara, I really liked Nicole, even though we didn't hang out much together. At the time I had other, closer friends, and she had a demanding live-in partner. But she was whip-smart and had a wicked sense of humor, which I thoroughly enjoyed. Then Nicole moved to Los Angeles, and instead of losing contact, we grew closer. I'd go stay with her in Los Angeles, and years later she inspired me to move to the big city myself.

At this point Nicole is an essential friend, someone who is truly a witness to my life story and I to hers. I think if, in those earlier years, I had asked myself, "Who will I still know in the decades to come?" I probably wouldn't have thought of Nicole. Yet here we are. The qualities that truly drew us together didn't become apparent to me until we didn't have proximity going for us. Then it became clear: *Here's someone I want to stay connected to—wherever we live!!*

BEYOND AN INSTANT CONNECTION

Years ago, when I was on college break and visiting my hometown, a high school friend asked if I'd be interested in going to a lecture with her on Aboriginal rights. I was. While we waited in the lecture theater, she introduced me to Sophie, a friend of hers from her own college. Sophie and I gabbed back and forth so spontaneously that by the time the lecture had begun, I'd invited her to visit me at school in Adelaide. Sophie came to visit and eventually transferred to my university.

Over time, Sophie and I shared houses, clothes, adventures, confidences with each other, and when I realized that she was terrible at keeping her monthly allowance in her pocket—she'd blow the whole wad in a few days leaving her broke for the rest of the month—I offered to be her banker. Sophie would give me her check, and I'd divvy out a weekly allocation. But it turned out that I was a softie and would cave in whenever she asked for extra cash. Another friend took over as banker and, I must say, she did a better job at it. All three of us are still friends today, decades and some seven thousand miles down the road.

So, there are people we spark to quickly and keep a long-term connection with. Yet I find these to be the rarest kinds of friendships. It's like a one-night stand turning into a marriage—it does happen, yet it's pretty unlikely. You need more than that first spark of attraction to sustain an enduring relationship.

For me, what makes an enduring relationship are the *small*, ongoing expressions of kindness, love, and compassion. Like the friend who treated John and me to a Rodriguez concert, after the three of us had watched *Searching for Sugar Man*, a poignant documentary about his life. Another long-term friend is someone who defended me to a couple of mutual friends, who were disparaging me behind my back. One close friend helped me declutter my storage area in the garage for a very small "friend's fee." And then there was the friend who shared her literary expertise with me, suggesting that—"just to get it out there"—I concentrate on one single idea from the first draft of what eventually became this book. These are not Kodak moments. They're not actions you can express with an emoji. These are generous deeds that elicit deep gratitude.

Here's a story that I think sums up a lovely gesture that resonated in my life for decades. In the 1980s, when Nora returned from Japan, she brought me back a traditional hanten jacket—a big, warm winter garment. She'd bought herself one in red and gave me one with glorious shimmery purple fabric on the outside, a deep, rich maroon inside, and a black velvet collar. The jacket was truly gorgeous, even though I didn't wear it much. I live in California where it's not that cold and given my body type, *ahem*, all that cotton padding made me look a little bit too bulky. However, it was a gift I valued, and it traveled with me to four cities and into eight different homes. Sometimes the coat hung in the back of my wardrobe, and at other times I'd display it on a wall. Every time I saw my hanten jacket, it reminded me of Nora and our friendship.

Scroll forward several decades. About a year ago, Nora was staying with me, and she bemoaned the fact that her daughter, Molly, had just returned from Japan without bringing Nora a new hanten jacket. After years of heavy use, Nora's red hanten jacket was threadbare, so she'd asked Molly to buy her a new one while she was in Japan—one that was *authentically* Japanese. But either Molly couldn't find such a jacket or else they got their wires crossed. Whatever the reason, it didn't happen.

So, I thought, *hmmm*. I said "Follow me." I led Nora to my bedroom closet, and from there I pulled out my traditional hanten coat that I had loved and kept for all these decades. "Do you mean this kind of coat?" I asked.

Nora's face lit up. "Yes," she said. "That's it!"

I told her, "You know what? I've had this all these years, and I feel as if I've been saving it for you. So, take it. It's yours!"

Nora took it from the hanger and gazed at it admiringly. Yes, this is exactly what she'd wanted.

And now, when I visit Nora on wintry days, I often see her wearing the coat as a dressing gown. Either that or it's hanging on the back of her bathroom door.

It's having this kind of history—one where we're spontaneous and loving, considerate and, when we can be, generous—that takes us beyond proximity and into what I consider to be the next level of friendship.

We all want to find ways to unfold the wonderful love we experience in our friendships. We have these moments with friends—sometimes quite challenging, other times inspiring—that are vital for our personal growth. I've learned to be less judgmental and kinder. Now I understand the impact of rejection or of misunderstanding an intention; I see how to overcome my bias by asking for a friend's perspective. I've discovered how important it is to set up honesty rules and protocols for sharing money, as well as knowing my boundaries so a friendship stays meaningful. And even if I disagree with a friend's opinion, I've learned to listen and ask follow-up questions. Listening is vital in a friendship, even if you don't always like what you're hearing.

As I quote my art teacher in chapter 12, there is so much more beauty in all the foreshortening and distortions, crags and folds, dark shadows and blotches than there is in the pretty picture that is our preconceived notion of what this *should* look like. That's the uniqueness of friendship. And what we explore in these relationships is what we can explore in our own selves.

These have been my lessons to learn: how to expand my knowledge to connect with the people I truly love, to acknowledge how they move me forward, and—hopefully—I them, on this beautiful path called life. This journey of friendship starts with me—becoming a better friend.

My thoughts on this are summed up by a lecture I recently heard by a monk, a teacher of Indian philosophy, who said, "I hear people complain, *I'm lonely!* and *Nobody loves me!*" He paused then, and he smiled. "Do they go out and love others?"

Therein lies the solution.

Acknowledgments

The process of creating and publishing a book is never a one-person effort, and this book on friendship, appropriately, took my friend community to put together. I am grateful for the support I have received all along the way.

I'd like to thank my editor, Margaret Bendet, for her incredible editorial skills and patience and for encouraging me to shift my focus toward something more personal and enduring.

Also, a big thanks to my science editor, Nolina Doud, who helped me navigate some complex science as well as locating specific studies when needed. I'm also grateful to the professors and coaches who graciously shared their research and insights with me.

To my agent, Anne Devlin, and the editorial, creative, and production team at Rowman & Littlefield, especially the senior executive editor Suzanne Staszak-Silva—I can't thank you all enough for believing in this book.

There are many close and loving friends I won't name here because they choose to remain anonymous—you know who you are because your stories appear in the book. Thank you to Angelica, Ken, Lisa, Lora, Malik, Robyn, Samantha, Steven, Susan, and William, who appear in the book under different names. I truly appreciate all of you for trusting me with your stories.

And to my Aussie friends, whom I've loved from afar for decades and who are featured in a number of stories—thank you for staying the course.

To the beta readers who generously reviewed an early version of the book: Jonathan Brady, Tiffany Credle-Crafton, Susanne Fest, Emily Flaherty—your contributions were invaluable.

To the dear monks who live in the monastery in the canyon and to my lovely women's group for your wisdom and caring.

To my amazing parents, Doreen and Jack, and my family for contributing so much to my life—especially Elaine for her big-hearted support for this book. And to John, the incredible person who shares my adventure on a daily basis; I love you.

Finally, I offer my heartfelt gratitude to my meditation teacher—thank you for generously providing deep insights and ongoing guidance.

Notes

CHAPTER 1

1. These studies are cited in an article by Tara Parker-Pope, "What Are Friends For? A Longer Life," *New York Times*, April 20, 2009, https://www.nytimes.com/2009/04/21/health/21well.html.

2. Sarah E. Hill and David M. Buss, "The Evolutionary Psychology of Envy," in *Envy: Theory and Research*, ed. R. Smith (New York: Oxford University Press, 2008), 60.

3. This statement is drawn from Rebecca G. Adams, a professor of sociology at the University of North Carolina–Greensboro, in the aforementioned article cited in note 1.

4. This was an insight from Jennifer L. Bevan (professor, Department of Communication Studies, Chapman University, California), Skype interview with the author, March 2015.

5. Rachel Martin, "In 'Together,' Former Surgeon General Writes about Importance of Human Contact," *NPR*, May 11, 2020, https://www.npr.org/sections/health-shots/2020/05/11/853308193/in-together-former-surgeon-general-writes-about-importance-of-human-connection.

6. John Cacioppo, "How Loneliness Begets Loneliness," interview by Olga Khazan, *The Atlantic*, April 6, 2017, https://www.theatlantic.com/health/archive/2017/04/how-loneliness-begets-loneliness/521841/.

7. The information on the unconscious mind was derived from two sources: Dr. Robert Williams's article "Processing Information with Nonconscious Mind," *Journal Psyche*, accessed February 13, 2020, http://journalpsyche.org/processing-information-with-nonconscious-mind/; and "Nonconscious," *AlleyDog.com*, January 22, 2020, https://www.alleydog.com/glossary/definition.php?term=Nonconscious.

CHAPTER 2

1. The four evolutionary psychologists cited are David M. G. Lewis, Laith Al-Shawaf, Eric M. Russell, and David M. Buss, "Friends and Happiness: An Evolutionary Perspective on Friendship," in *Friendship and Happiness: Across the Life-Span and Cultures*, ed. Meliksah Demur (New York: Springer, 2015), 37–57, https://doi.org/10.1007/978-94-017-9603-3_3.

2. Peter DeScioli and Robert Kurzban, "The Alliance Hypothesis for Human Friendship," *Public Library of Science ONE* 4, no. 6 (2009): e5802, https://doi.org/10.1371/journal.pone.0005802.

3. Oren Jay Sofer, *Say What You Mean: A Mindful Approach to Nonviolent Communication* (Boulder, CO: Shambhala Publications, 2018), 73.

CHAPTER 3

1. Matthew B. Kugler (associate professor, Northwestern Pritzker School of Law, Illinois), Skype interview with the author, April 2016.

2. Emily Pronin and Matthew B. Kugler, "Valuing Thoughts, Ignoring Behavior: The Introspection Illusion as a Source of the Bias Blind Spot," *Journal of Experimental Social Psychology* 43, no. 4 (2007): 565–78, https://doi.org/10.1016/j.jesp.2006.05.011.

3. Nicholas Epley, *Mindwise: How We Understand What Others Think, Believe, Feel, and Want* (New York: Alfred A. Knopf, 2014), 173.

4. These are two resources for the minimal group paradigm: Henri Tajfel "Experiments in Intergroup Discrimination," *Scientific American* 223 (1970): 96–102; and Henri Tajfel, Michael G. Billig, R. P. Bundy, and Claude Flament, "Social Categorization and Intergroup Behaviour," abstract, *European Journal of Social Psychology* 1, no. 2 (1971): 149–78, https://doi.org/10.1002/ejsp.2420010202.

CHAPTER 4

1. At the time of this writing, I find *very* few relationship-related studies cited by *any* psychologists, including evolutionary researchers, that include anyone who identifies as or with LGBTQ+. More focus on these underrepresented groups would add immeasurable value to the understanding of our species.

2. Sarah E. Hill and David M. Buss, "The Evolutionary Psychology of Envy," in *Envy: Theory and Research*, ed. R. Smith (New York: Oxford University Press, 2008), 65–66.

3. Ibid., 68.

4. A research study by Kristina M. Durante, Vladas Griskevicius, Stephanie M. Cantú, and Jeffrey A. Simpson, "Money, Status, and the Ovulatory Cycle," *Journal of Marketing Research* 51, no. 1 (2014): 34, https://doi.org/10.1509/jmr.11.0327.

5. Ibid., 27–39.

6. Kristina M. Durante (associate professor, Rutgers Business School, New Jersey), Skype interview with the author, February 2016.

7. Jaime M. Cloud (associate professor, Western Oregon University, Oregon), Skype interview with the author, February 2016.

8. This statistic is from a research paper by Kristina M. Durante, Vladas Griskevicius, Sarah E. Hill, Carin Perilloux, and Norman P. Li, "Ovulation, Female Competition, and Product Choice: Hormonal Influences on Consumer Behavior," *Journal of Consumer Research* 37, no. 6 (2011): 921, https://doi.org/10.1086/656575.

CHAPTER 5

1. Jennifer L. Bevan, "Understanding the Role of Intrapersonal Uncertainty in the Experience and Expression of Jealousy in Cross-Sex Friendships" (master's thesis, University of Delaware, 1999), https://www.communication.udel.edu/MA%20Theses/bevan.pdf.

2. Jennifer L. Bevan, *The Communication of Jealousy* (New York: Peter Lang, 2013).

3. Jennifer L. Bevan (professor, Department of Communication Studies, Chapman University, California), Skype interview with the author, March 2015.

4. A study by Timothy R. Worley and Jennifer Samp, "Exploring the Associations between Relational Uncertainty, Jealousy about Partner's Friendships, and Jealousy Expression in Dating Relationships," *Communication Studies* 65, no. 4 (2014): 370–88, https://doi.org/10.1080/10510974.2013.833529.

5. Timothy Worley's study, coauthored with Jennifer Samp, researched different forms of jealousy we experience when our romantic partner has a close friend. "Friendship Characteristics, Threat Appraisals, and Varieties of Jealousy

About Romantic Partners' Friendships," *Interpersona* 8, no. 2 (2014): 231–44, https://doi.org/10.5964/ijpr.v8i2.169.

6. David T. Hsu, Benjamin J. Sanford, Kortni K. Meyers, Tiffany M. Love, Kathleen E. Hazlett, Heng Wang, Lisong Ni, Sara J. Walker, Brian J. Mickey, Steven T. Korycinski, Robert A. Koeppe, Jennifer K. Crocker, Scott A. Langenecker, and Jon-Kar Zubieta, "Response of the μ-opioid System to Social Rejection and Acceptance," *Molecular Psychiatry* 18, no. 11 (November 2013): 1211–17, https://doi.org/10.1038/mp.2013.96.

7. David T. Hsu (assistant professor of Psychiatry, Renaissance School of Medicine, Stony Brook University, New York), Skype interview with the author, August 2014 and November 2019.

8. A later study conducted by David Hsu's research team shows how rejection is experienced in the brains of people who are clinically depressed—and why it's difficult for them to shake off social pain. David T. Hsu, Benjamin J. Sanford, Kortni K. Meyers, Tiffany M. Love, Kathleen E. Hazlett, Sara J. Walker, Brian J. Mickey, Robert A. Koeppe, Scott A. Langenecker, and Jon-Kar Zubieta, "It Still Hurts: Altered Endogenous Opioid Activity in the Brain During Social Rejection and Acceptance in Major Depressive Disorder," *Molecular Psychiatry* 20, no. 2 (February 2015): 193–200, https://doi.org/10.1038/mp.2014.185.

CHAPTER 6

1. Kelton Global conducted an online study for Fidelity Investments surveying 1,542 females who were eighteen years and older. A summary of the study's results was published as "The Fidelity Investments Money FIT Women Study: Executive Summary," *Fidelity Investments*, 2015, https://www.fidelity.com/bin-public/060_www_fidelity_com/documents/women-fit-money-study.pdf.

2. Survey Methodology: "The survey questionnaire was written by Acorns [an investment app firm] and conducted from November 11, 2017, through December 1, 2017, using SurveyMonkey's nationally representative online research panel. The sample population consisted of 3,010 Americans, comprised of 1,576 females and 1,434 males between 18–44, across the following segments: 1,000 respondents aged 18–24, 1,007 respondents aged 25–34 and 1,003 respondents aged 35–44." The survey results were published as the "2017 Money Matters Report," *Acorns*, January 2018, https://sqy7rm.media.zestyio.com/Acorns2017_MoneyMattersReport.pdf.

3. Elizabeth Dunn and Michael Norton, *Happy Money: The Science of Smarter Spending* (New York: Simon & Schuster, 2013), 10–11.

4. Ibid., 56.

5. Online article on Finder (an informational financial website), Olivia Chow, "Americans Owe an Estimated $184 Billion to Friends and Family Annually," *Finder*, June 28, 2018, https://www.finder.com/americans-borrow -friends-and-family-household-debt.

6. Dunn and Norton, *Happy Money*, 116.

7. Linda Dezsö and George Loewenstein, "Lenders' Blind Trust and Borrowers' Blind Spots: A Descriptive Investigation of Personal Loans," *Journal of Economic Psychology* 33, no. 5 (2012): 996–1011, https://doi.org/10.1016/j .joep.2012.06.002.

8. Ibid., 1000. The survey sample was taken in the United States, and the researchers concentrated on the 654 borrowers and lenders who were friends, coworkers, siblings, or cousins: "The survey, which was fielded in 2011, recruited respondents from the Amazon.com service MTurk. Amazon MTurk is a marketplace on which people register to complete diverse types of computer-based tasks, including completing surveys, in exchange for remuneration . . . symmetric loans were made between borrowers and lenders who were similar in demographic characteristics, including age in years (lenders' mean = 32.0, SD = 11.1 and borrowers' mean = 31.4, SD = 10.8), gender (both groups approximately 61% female), racial composition and education. There were slightly more borrowers than lenders in the lowest income strata (11.9% lenders versus 17.7% borrowers) and slightly more part-time employed people than full employed among borrowers than lenders. The survey, which was administered on Qualtrics and included informed consent, took an average of about 20 min to complete. . . . In each case, participants were asked about the most recent loan they had been involved within the past 5 years. The lending and borrowing sections of the survey contained equivalent questions. For example, in the lending survey, respondents were asked 'To whom did you lend the money?' whereas in the borrowing phase, respondents were asked 'Who gave you the loan?'"

9. Ibid., 1006.

10. Linda Dezsö (assistant professor, Faculty of Business, Economics and Statistics, University of Vienna, Austria), Skype interview with the author, October 2014.

11. Sharon Cox, a financial professional and certified financial planner for twenty-eight years, provides one-on-one and small group money coaching and interactive workshops for women through her business, The Money Dance. She

has a master's degree from Indiana State University and a certificate of advanced study with a focus on teacher training from the University of Chicago; Skype interview with the author, April 2018.

CHAPTER 7

1. Scott H. Eidelman (associate professor, Department of Psychological Science, University of Arkansas), Skype interview with the author, April 2015.

2. Scott Eidelman, Jennifer Pattershall, and Christian S. Crandall, "Longer Is Better," *Journal of Experimental Social Psychology* 46, no. 4 (November 2010): 993–98, https://doi.org/10.1016/j.jesp.2010.07.008.

3. Geoffrey Greif, "The Impact of Divorce on Friendships with Couples and Individuals: What Happens with Couple Friendships after Divorce?" *Psychology Today*, September 6, 2012, https://www.psychologytoday.com/us/blog/buddy-system/201209/the-impact-divorce-friendships-couples-and-individuals.

4. Chip Heath and Dan Heath, *Switch: How to Change Things When Change Is Hard* (New York: Broadway Books, 2010), 47–48.

CHAPTER 8

1. Sara Schairer (executive director of the nonprofit organization Compassion It), "What's the Difference Between Empathy, Sympathy, and Compassion?" *Chopra Center*, November 23, 2019, https://chopra.com/articles/whats-the-difference-between-empathy-sympathy-and-compassion.

2. Dacher Keltner, "Darwin's Touch: Survival of the Kindest—Happy Birthday, Darwin," *Psychology Today*, February 11, 2009, https://www.psychologytoday.com/us/blog/born-be-good/200902/darwins-touch-survival-the-kindest.

3. Charles Darwin, *The Descent of Man, and Selection in Relation to Sex* (London: John Murray, 1871).

4. Keltner, "Darwin's Touch."

5. Steve W. Cole (professor, UCLA School of Medicine), "Ming-Wu Lecture," November 12, 2013, CCARE School of Medicine, Stanford University, 28:28, https://www.bing.com/videos/search?q=Steve+Cole+ucla&view=detail&mid=8F22298E0C07EFC1645C8F22298E0C07EFC1645C&FORM=VIRE.

6. Barbara L. Fredrickson, Karen M. Grewen, Kimberly A. Coffey, Sara B. Algoe, Ann M. Firestine, Jesusa M. G. Arevalo, Jeffrey Ma, and Steven W. Cole, "A Functional Genomic Perspective on Human Well-Being," *PNAS* 110, no. 33 (August 2013): 13684–89, https://doi.org/10.1073/pnas.1305419110.

For this study, eighty-four healthy adults were recruited to measure both hedonic and eudaemonic well-being—for example, here are some questions they asked: "*How often do you feel . . . happy?* (hedonic), *satisfied?* (hedonic), *that your life has a sense of direction, or meaning to it?* (eudaemonic), *that you have experiences that challenge you to grow and become a better person?* (eudaemonic), *that you had something to contribute to society?* (eudaemonic)"

Participants self-reported their observations, first through their conscious and psychological observations—and gave blood samples to measure adversity at the molecular level (high inflammation, low immunity—did they feel threatened) through their gene expression.

This is where it gets interesting: both hedonic and eudaemonic showed high levels of happiness at the psychological level—conscious emotional experiences. However, the study found that the participants who expressed eudaemonic happiness had *favorable* gene expressions—feeling safe, not threatened, whereas, hedonic participants showed *unfavorable* gene expression—higher threat response, and inflammation.

7. Veronique de Turenne, "The Pain of Chronic Loneliness Can Be Detrimental to Your Health," *UCLA Newsroom*, December 21, 2016, http://newsroom.ucla.edu/stories/stories-20161206.

8. Steve W. Cole, "The Psychophysiology of Compassion," January 28, 2015, Panel presentation at CCARE, Stanford University, The Science of Compassion 2014 conference, 17:17, https://www.youtube.com/watch?v=VAL-MMYptQc.

9. Ibid., 16:55.

CHAPTER 9

1. Jason S. Moser, Rachel Hartwig, Tim P. Moran, Alexander A. Jendrusina, and Ethan Kross, "Neural Markers of Positive Reappraisal and Their Associations with Trait Reappraisal and Worry," *Journal of Abnormal Psychology* 123, no. 1 (February 2014): 91–105, https://doi.org/10.1037/a0035817.

2. Jason S. Moser (associate professor, Department of Psychology, Michigan State University), Skype interview with the author, May 2015 and March 2020.

CHAPTER 10

1. Timothy R. Levine (professor and chair, Department of Communication Studies, the University of Alabama at Birmingham), Skype interview with the author, June 2016.

2. Timothy Levine, "Truth-Default Theory (TDT): A Theory of Human Deception and Deception Detection," *Journal of Language and Social Psychology* 33, no. 4 (May 23, 2014): 378–92, https://doi.org/10.1177/0261927X14535916.

3. Steven A. McCornack (professor, Department of Communication Studies, the University of Alabama at Birmingham), Skype interview with the author, June 2016.

4. Steven A. McCornack, Kelly Morrison, Jihyun Esther Paik, Amy M. Wisner, and Xun Zhu, "Information Manipulation Theory 2: A Propositional Theory of Deceptive Discourse Production," *Journal of Language and Social Psychology* 33, no. 4 (June 4, 2014): 348–77, https://doi.org/10.1177/0261927X14534656.

5. Andrew Scott, "'Sherlock Has Changed My Whole Career': Andrew Scott Interview," interview by James Rampton, *Independent*, November 15, 2013, https://www.independent.co.uk/arts-entertainment/tv/features/sherlock-has-changed-my-whole-career-andrew-scott-interview-8940114.html.

CHAPTER 11

1. Barry Collodi (PhD in psychology, University of Colorado, executive coach specializing in corporate team-building—from interpersonal skills to organizational communication and leadership), recorded interview with the author, October 2014.

2. David M. G. Lewis, Daniel Conroy-Beam, Laith Al-Shawaf, Annia Raja, Todd DeKay, and David M. Buss, "Friends with Benefits: The Evolved Psychology of Same- and Opposite-Sex Friendship," *Evolutionary Psychology* 9, no. 4 (2011): 544, https://doi.org/10.1177/147470491100900407.

3. Ibid., 547.

4. Tamas David-Barrett, Anna Rotkirch, James Carney, Isabel Behncke Izquierdo, Jamie A. Krems, Dylan Townley, Elinor McDaniell, Anna Byrne-Smith, and Robin I. M. Dunbar, "Women Favour Dyadic Relationships, but

Men Prefer Clubs: Cross-Cultural Evidence from Social Networking," *PLOS ONE* 10, no. 3 (March 2015), https://doi.org/10.1371/journal.pone.0118329.

5. Paul H. Wright and Mary Beth Scanlon, "Gender Role Orientations and Friendship: Some Attenuation, But Gender Differences Abound," *Sex Roles* 24, no. 9–10 (May 1991): 552. https://doi.org/10.1007/BF00288413.

6. Ibid., 565.

7. These questions were adapted from Margarita Tartakovsky's suggestions in her article, "7 Tips for Setting Boundaries At Work," *PsychCentral*, 2014, updated 2018, https://psychcentral.com/blog/7-tips-for-setting-boundaries-at -work/.

CHAPTER 12

1. National Public Radio social science correspondent and *Hidden Brain* host Shankar Vedantam, "People Like People Who Ask Questions," interview by Steve Inskeep and Rachel Martin, *Morning Edition*, NPR, radio broadcast, November 29, 2017 (5:19 a.m. ET). This interview's transcript was published on NPR's *Hidden Brain: A Conversation About Life's Patterns*, https://www.npr .org/2017/11/29/567133944/people-like-people-who-ask-questions.

2. A study on follow-up questions by Karen Huang, Michael Yeomans, Alison Wood Brooks, Julia Minson, and Francesca Gino, "It Doesn't Hurt to Ask: Question-Asking Increases Liking," *Journal of Personality and Social Psychology* 113, no. 3 (2017): 430–52, https://doi.org/10.1037/pspi0000097.

3. Ibid., 438.

4. Alison Wood Brooks, "People Will Like You More If You Start Asking Followup Questions," interview by Rachel Layne, *Forbes*, October 30, 2017, https://www.forbes.com/sites/hbsworkingknowledge/2017/10/30/people -will-like-you-more-if-you-start-asking-followup-questions/.

5. Shelly L. Gable, Gian C. Gonzaga, and Amy Strachman, "Will You Be There for Me When Things Go Right? Supportive Responses to Positive Event Disclosures," *Journal of Personality and Social Psychology* 91, no. 5 (2006): 904–17, https://doi.org/10.1037/0022-3514.91.5.904.

6. Ibid., 906.

7. Ibid., 914.

CHAPTER 13

1. David T. Hsu (assistant professor of Psychiatry, Renaissance School of Medicine, Stony Brook University, New York), Skype interview with the author, August 2014 and November 2019.

2. David T. Hsu, Benjamin J. Sanford, Kortni K. Meyers, Tiffany M. Love, Kathleen E. Hazlett, Heng Wang, Lisong Ni, Sara J. Walker, Brian J. Mickey, Steven T. Korycinski, Robert A. Koeppe, Jennifer K. Crocker, Scott A. Langenecker, and Jon-Kar Zubieta, "Response of the μ-Opioid System to Social Rejection and Acceptance," *Molecular Psychiatry* 18, no. 11 (November 2013): 1211–17, https://doi.org/10.1038/mp.2013.96.

Note: Researchers use Cyberball to observe neural, cognitive, and psychological responses to social exclusion. The person thinks that they're playing with other participants, but are instead playing with preprogrammed avatars. The researchers track how the participant responds when included in the game—social inclusion—and when they are excluded—social exclusion—as well as other variables. While some studies use psychological markers, like self-reports before and after the game, other studies use physiological and neural markers, like pupil dilation and neuroimaging measures.

3. Robin Dunbar, *Wikipedia*, accessed September 28, 2020, https://en.wikipedia.org/wiki/Robin_Dunbar.

4. R. I. M. Dunbar, "Do Online Social Media Cut through the Constraints that Limit the Size of Offline Social Networks?" *Royal Society Open Science* 3, no. 1 (January 2016): 1, https://doi.org/10.1098/rsos.150292.

5. Ibid., 6.

6. Tim Adams, "Interview [with] Sherry Turkle: 'I Am Not Anti-Technology, I Am Pro-Conversation,'" *The Guardian*, October 18, 2015, https://www.theguardian.com/science/2015/oct/18/sherry-turkle-not-anti-technology-pro-conversation.

7. Dunbar, "Do Online Social Media," 6–7.

8. Ibid., 1.

9. Sherry Turkle, *Reclaiming Conversation: The Power of Talk in a Digital Age* (New York: Penguin Publishing Group, 2015), 4.

10. Danilo Bzdok and Robin I. M. Dunbar, "The Neurobiology of Social Distance," *Trends in Cognitive Sciences* 24, no. 9 (September 2020): 722, https://doi.org/10.1016/j.tics.2020.05.016.

11. April Bleske-Rechek's advice is noted in Cari Romm's article, "How to Keep a Long-Distance Friendship Alive," "The Cut," *New York Magazine*,

May 7, 2017, https://www.thecut.com/2017/03/how-to-keep-a-long-distance -friendship-alive.html.

CHAPTER 14

1. The material on follow-up questions is from a study by Karen Huang, Michael Yeomans, Alison Wood Brooks, Julia Minson, and Francesca Gino, "It Doesn't Hurt to Ask: Question-Asking Increases Liking," *Journal of Personality and Social Psychology* 113, no. 3 (2017): 438–439, https://doi.org/10.1037/ pspi0000097.

2. Barry Collodi (PhD in psychology, University of Colorado, executive coach specializing in corporate team-building—from interpersonal skills to organizational communication and leadership), recorded interview with the author, October 2014.

3. Jason S. Moser, Adrienne Dougherty, Whitney I. Mattson, Benjamin Katz, Tim P. Moran, Darwin Guevarra, Holly Shablack, Ozlem Ayduk, John Jonides, Marc G. Berman, and Ethan Kross, "Third-Person Self-Talk Facilitates Emotion Regulation without Engaging Cognitive Control: Converging Evidence from ERP and fMRI," *Scientific Reports* 7, no. 1 (July 3, 2017): 1–9, https://doi.org/10.1038/s41598-017-04047-3.

4. Psychologist Ethan Kross explains third-person self-talk in an article by Pamela Weintraub, "The Voice of Reason," *Psychology Today*, May 4, 2015, https://www.psychologytoday.com/articles/201505/the-voice-reason.

5. Jason S. Moser (associate professor, Department of Psychology, Michigan State University), Skype interview with the author, May 2015 and March 2020.

6. The self-talk study Jason Moser referred to is by Ethan Kross, Emma Bruehlman-Senecal, Jiyoug Park, Aleah Burson, Adrienne Dougherty, Holly Shablack, Ryan Bremner, Ozlem Ayduk, and Jason Moser, "Self-Talk as a Regulatory Mechanism: How You Do It Matters," *Journal of Personality and Social Psychology* 106, no. 2 (February 2014): 304–24, https://doi.org/10.1037/ a0035173.

CHAPTER 15

1. Allie Volpe, "Why You Need a Network of Low-Stakes, Casual Friendships," *New York Times*, May 6, 2019.

2. Mark S. Granovetter originated the theory of weak ties, which he presents in his study "The Strength of Weak Ties," *American Journal of Sociology* 78, no. 6 (May 1, 1973):1360–80, https://doi.org/10.1086/225469. His theory is discussed further in Mark Granovetter, "The Strength of Weak Ties: A Network Theory Revisited," *Sociological Theory* 1 (1983): 201–33, https://doi.org/10.2307/202051.

3. The study cited in the *New York Times* article researching the relational links of weak ties to feelings of happiness and a sense of belonging is by Gillian M. Sandstrom and Elizabeth W. Dunn, "Social Interactions and Well-Being: The Surprising Power of Weak Ties," *Personality and Social Psychology Bulletin* 40, no. 7 (2014): 910–22, https://doi.org/10.1177/0146167214529799.

4. The findings of social psychologist Leon Festinger's propinquity studies are summarized in "Leon Festinger," *Wikipedia*, accessed May 15, 2019, https://en.wikipedia.org/wiki/Leon_Festinger#cite_note-45.

5. Richard L. Moreland and Scott R. Beach, "Exposure effects in the classroom: The development of affinity among students," abstract, *Journal of Experimental Social Psychology* 28, no. 3 (May 1992): 255–76, https://doi.org/10.1016/0022-1031(92)90055-O.

6. Researchers tracking nearly twenty years of social connection discover that "The modal respondent now reports having no confidant; the modal respondent in 1985 had three confidants. Both kin and non-kin confidants were lost in the past two decades, but the greater decrease of non-kin ties leads to more confidant networks centered on spouses and parents, with fewer contacts through voluntary associations and neighborhoods." These findings are reported in Miller McPherson, Lynn Smith-Lovin, and Matthew E. Brashears, "Social Isolation in America: Changes in Core Discussion Networks Over Two Decades," abstract, *American Sociological Review* 71, no. 3 (2006): 353–75, https://doi.org/10.1177/000312240607100301.

Please note: Since this study was published, there has been some discussion around a coding error in one question asked of participants in 2004, which influenced the metrics in the overall outcome. Even so, I have included it; I think it's a rigorous study that adds to the overall point that we are losing our close connections. For further reading on the General Social Survey (GSS), visit the official website at https://gss.norc.org/.

7. Eric Klinenberg, "Is There Really a 'Loneliness Epidemic'?" episode 407, interview by Stephen J. Dubner, *Freakonomics Radio*, Stitcher and Dubner Productions, February 26, 2020, https://freakonomics.com/podcast/loneliness/.

8. On the *Freakonomics Radio* episode on loneliness, Eric Klinenberg, a sociology professor at New York University, explored why so many people died during a heat wave in Chicago in 1995. In his first book about the Chicago heat wave, he discovered that one of the most important risk factors leading to death was that people were living alone—since there had been "the rise of the one-person household." Following this line of research in his second book, Klinenberg studied people who lived alone and discovered that "the choice to live alone does not necessarily create loneliness," and that people living alone were "surprisingly social." Even so, I think it will be interesting if future studies explore how people living alone during the COVID-19 pandemic adapted to sheltering in place using multiple internet platforms. Will these new methods of communication be enough to maintain a high level of sociability and, consequently, well-being?

Bibliography

Bell, Sandra, and Simon Coleman, eds. *The Anthropology of Friendship*. Oxford, UK: Berg, 1999.

Cacioppo, John T., and William Patrick. *Loneliness: Human Nature and the Need for Social Connection*. New York: W. W. Norton & Company, 2008.

Duhigg, Charles. *The Power of Habit: Why We Do What We Do in Life and Business*. New York: Random House, 2012.

Dunn, Elizabeth, and Michael Norton. *Happy Money: The Science of Smarter Spending*. New York: Simon & Schuster, 2013.

Dweck, Carol S. *Mindset: The New Psychology of Success*. New York: Ballantine Books, 2007.

Epley, Nicholas. *Mindwise: How We Understand What Others Think, Believe, Feel, and Want*. New York: Alfred A. Knopf, 2014.

Gottman, John M., and Nan Silva. *The Seven Principles for Making Marriage Work: A Practical Guide from the Country's Foremost Relationship Expert*. 2nd ed. New York: Harmony Books, 2015.

Heath, Chip, and Dan Heath. *Switch: How to Change Things When Change Is Hard*. New York: Broadway Books, 2010.

Herbert, Wray. *On Second Thought: Outsmarting Your Mind's Hard-Wired Habits*. New York: Crown Publishers, 2010.

Meadows, Donella H., and Diana Wright. *Thinking in Systems: A Primer*. White River Junction, VT: Chelsea Green Publishing, 2008.

Sofer, Oren Jay. *Say What You Mean: A Mindful Approach to Nonviolent Communication*. Boulder, CO: Shambhala Publications, 2018.

Index

About the Author

Glenda D. Shaw has worked for more than twenty-five years as a producer for talk television and radio shows in Los Angeles and New York for companies including Viacom, King World, and MTV. Nominated for two Daytime Emmys for producing and writing, she is a member of the Writers Guild of America, the Producers Guild of America, and the National Academy of Television Arts and Sciences. She has also written for magazines, including *LA Style*.